SHE
REIGNS

SHE REIGNS

CONQUERING YOUR TRIGGERS, FEARS, AND WORRIES WITH GOD'S TRUTH

TARAH-LYNN SAINT-ELLEN

Revell

a division of Baker Publishing Group
Grand Rapids, Michigan

Published by Revell
a division of Baker Publishing Group
PO Box 6287, Grand Rapids, MI 49516-6287
www.revellbooks.com

Printed in the United States of America

Library of Congress Cataloging-in-Publication Data
Names: Saint-Elien, Tarah-Lynn, author.
Title: She reigns : conquering your triggers, fears, and worries with God's truth / Tarah-Lynn Saint-Elien.
Description: Grand Rapids, MI : Revell, a division of Baker Publishing Group, [2023] | Includes bibliographical references.
Identifiers: LCCN 2022035711 | ISBN 9780800736972 (paperback) | ISBN 9780800742881 (casebound) | ISBN 9781493439782 (ebook)
Subjects: LCSH: Christian women—Religious life. | Self-confidence—Religious aspects—Christianity. | Fear—Religious Aspects—Christianity. | Worry—Religious aspects—Christianity. | Anxiety—Religious aspects—Christianity.
Classification: LCC BV4527 .S2255 2023 | DDC 248.8/43—dc23/eng/20220826
LC record available at https://lccn.loc.gov/2022035711

This book contains original material as well as excerpts from *Claim Your Crown* by Tarah-Lynn Saint-Elien, published by Revell Books, 2020.

The Proprietor is represented by the literary agency of Credo Communications, LLC, Grand Rapids, Michigan, www.credocommunications.net.

Baker Publishing Group publications use paper produced from sustainable forestry practices and post-consumer waste whenever possible.

23 24 25 26 27 28 29   7 6 5 4 3 2 1

To my grandmother, Marie Fleurmond

The enemy has lost the victory over your mind. Alzheimer's will not rob you. God has not forgotten about you or your faith that inspires generations. Like Mom has said, "If it weren't for you, Tarah-Lynn wouldn't be telling the world about Jesus." Thank you for fighting for our family and introducing us all to the greatest love we will ever come to know.

CONTENTS

A LOVE NOTE

Hey friend,

If you are struggling with constant anxiety, sadness, and/or harmful thoughts, I want you to know that I see you, I love you, and I am not simplifying your pain. Some healing processes take more than a couple of steps. I may not understand all your struggles, but I do know there is a reason why you are here on this earth: you have purpose. And I pray I can encourage you to never give up. While I don't have all the answers to your pain, I'm proud of you for being here and seeking solutions in God. I believe He has given us community, therapists, and doctors, as well as spiritual ministers of healing to aid with deliverance. I also believe this book operates in the healing realm. The restoring power and the truth of God is imminent. With this book, I pray that you feel the love of God ricocheting off the pages, tearing down every lie the enemy feeds you. I pray you don't feel alone in your thoughts as I declare to you that the Lord is near and tending to you right where you are. He loves you and His intent is always to see you live free.

Tarah-Lynn Saint-Elien

INTRODUCTION

When I first had the idea for *She Reigns*, I hadn't a clue of the life experiences I would be able to write about. I wasn't consciously struggling with my emotions and a battle of the mind. Then, tragedy after tragedy hit—and all within a couple of months. I looked up to my ceiling and wryly said, "Well, thanks for the content, God!"

I should've expected it. Almost a year prior, I had the revelation that when I publish a new book, severe trials related to the very encouragement I've shared come at me full force.

Take my first book, *Claim Your Crown*, for instance. It was released a few weeks before the COVID-19 pandemic began, and while it served as a resource for how to grow confidence in Christ, it was also accompanied by an attack on my own identity. I, the woman who was taught I was royalty since birth, felt myself shrinking back. I almost muzzled my God-given message because I struggled with the weight of what I had to offer; it didn't feel like it mattered. I found it cringeworthy to talk about my book when our whole world had been disrupted—my mind felt disrupted.

I stepped back for a little bit and limited my time on social media. I'm prudent when it comes to posting, and I didn't want to be influenced by the panic the world was feeling. I went into hiding, bringing my thoughts along as a pillow and the unfamiliar feelings as a thermal blanket. But man, I was cold.

God has a funny way of getting us back to where we need to be. While I was preparing to change the course of sharing my heart behind the book, I recalled how the Spanish word *corona* translates to *crown* in English. And my mother pounded it in my head daily: now more than ever, God's heirs need to rise up and claim their crowns. My perspective changed.

Later came the *Love Letters from the King* devotional. I wrote it so readers would know how much they are treasured and how our heavenly Father cares about the details of our lives. I produced a special promotional video featuring my army of sisters around the globe to further illustrate how God's love and His answers reach His daughters wherever they are in the world.

I created a script, made a call for submissions online, and in droves, received submissions with these women reciting,

> Dear God,
> Can You see me?
> Do You hear me?
> What do You call me?

Do You really even love me?
Do You care?
Are You even there?

Dear reader, can you guess what happened next? A few months after that release, I was tested in every single theme I presented!

Like you, I have felt overlooked and hidden from God. Like you, I have felt He doesn't hear me or that He actually enjoys sending me radio silence as a response. Like you, I have desperately wanted to tangibly feel His love and have felt nothing. Like you, I've gotten angry at God and told Him if He cared at all, I wouldn't be suffering with this intense measure—that He was the perpetrator inflicting me with all this pain. And like you, I've asked Him, "Where are You?" Although my life has been filled with struggles and heartbreak, I've never questioned God's existence. But the past few years have been overwhelmingly challenging. Like the poem those women shared, I found myself asking God, "Are You even there?"

I'm in a different place now than I was then, a healthier one. But allow me to take you back to 2020—when the enemy was aiming for me to lose my mind. God helped me gain something so much better: a renewed mentality. A kingdom mindset.

It's possible you're at a place where a message at an online service isn't enough to get you through the day. Perhaps you feel God is too late to rescue you. But will you allow me to be that vessel that shows you otherwise? Maybe you'll resonate with the lessons I learned in my own mess and hear God for yourself. If you give this book a chance, you'll see that while you lost the strength to look for answers, the Truth sought you.

It's easy to believe the evidence that supports the thoughts running rampant in our minds: *I won't ever be satisfied. My enemies are winning—I'm not. God must've changed His mind, or maybe He just forgot about me* . . . But it is pivotal to speak God's promises in spite of what you see and feel. So with this book, we're not going to reject reality; we're going to relearn faith.

She Reigns was birthed through a heavy-hitting testing ground like no other. My emotions and my mind worked against me. I had to *fight* for my heart to be open and to choose victory in my mind. I haven't only experienced these blows, I have overcome them, and I'm excited to show you how you can, too.

You'll be guided through the truths and tools needed to take negative thoughts and debilitating emotions captive so you are able to posture your heart for delight, overcome the orphan-and-poverty mindset, and accept our King's view as supreme over what you see. Once you identify your triggers, fears, and worries, you'll be ready to combat them with God's thoughts toward you.

This book isn't dedicated to convincing you that you're royalty. (That's what *Claim Your Crown* is for!) Sure, we will definitely discuss that how you see yourself affects the way you think—but *She Reigns* exists to help you learn how that crown you have can also double as a helmet. You can indeed allow the peace that surpasses all understanding to reign over your mind.

By reflecting on my own experiences and studying the successes and failures of biblical queens, I aim to provide refreshing hope and help for the woman ready to rewire her thoughts—and, as a result, reign effectively with kingdom-mindedness. Together, we'll pinpoint the negative thought patterns, address the root of the issue, and seek Scripture for practical takeaways. This book will give you the framework to overcome and live free.

I encourage you to take your time reading, to sit with the words, and to participate in the reflection questions at the end of the chapters. I want you to feel *all* the feels and to think on the messages God is getting across to you. It'll be a lot of heart work, but it'll also be a fun time. It's kind of weird that I'm giddy right now, but I'm thrilled to be transparent in this way! I have a few confessions that I'll be letting you in on. Some shocking, some uncomfortable—but all of them reveal my honest fears, doubts, and worries. All this to illustrate to you that doubt can be necessary for growth. Your anger and confusion can be used, too. God welcomes your questions and the feelings you're terrified to share with those you love most.

After I share these confessions, I'll lead you to combat, and then I'll offer resources you need to adjust your crown. To do this, I've taken some pages out of my diary and have repurposed them for you. You may not understand all of me and my lived experiences, but I am honored to open my heart in book form, to be allowed a space where you can see me, you can see yourself, and you can see God.

In the past, we've claimed our crowns and soaked in the love letters from our King, so what are we to do now? Well, queen, I'll show you how to reign.

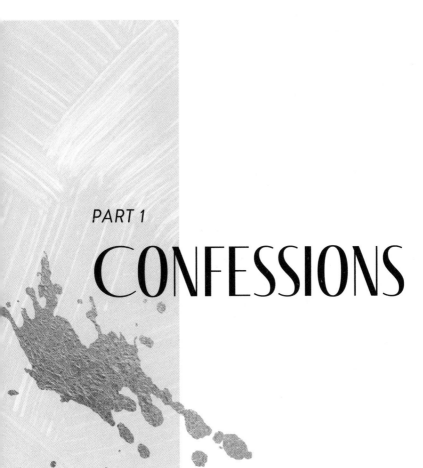

PART 1

CONFESSIONS

1

Confessions and the Crown of Life

Disrupting Fear and Drawing a True Picture of God

There is no fear in love. But perfect love drives out fear, because fear has to do with punishment. The one who fears is not made perfect in love.

1 John 4:18 NIV

Confession #1: I initially became a Christian because I was terrified of the rapture and the final judgment—not because I was *so* in love with Jesus and couldn't do life without Him. Sure, I was aware that as a sinner, I needed Christ as a Savior, but that's not why I chose Him.

I grew up in a Christian household where I was reminded that I am a daughter of the King and my Father's love was always available to me. My earthly dad is a devoted deacon, and my mom, though ill and in chronic pain, always finds the most incomparable joy in the Lord.

As Proverbs 22:6 says, they raised me and my siblings in the ways in which we should go.

I was taught to revere God, and I sincerely did. I prayed when I remembered to during the day and (mandatorily) joined nightly family prayer in my parents' bedroom or the living room. There was church every Sunday, Bible study on Wednesdays, and choir practice every Saturday. I didn't have a secret life, but I wasn't perfect. I did all I was "supposed" to do and kept Christ at the center, as church culture encouraged . . . but He still didn't have my whole heart.

Fear-based faith was the culprit. Back then, faith to me was, "If you don't follow this list of rules, surely you're on a highway to hell." I saw a loving but moody God peering down from His throne, awaiting the best moments to punish me here on earth and lock me out of heaven when the time came. I understood He was both a merciful Father and a righteous judge, but I believed the scale tipped over to the condemning side *way* more. That was the God I chose to live for . . . because at least He was better than hell.

Watching the *Left Behind* series at a youth group session probably ignited the flame of fear for me. If you haven't seen it, it's a movie series that depicts the destruction and havoc that goes on after Jesus returns for His children and brings them to heaven. The people who are left behind have to suffer through life with their saved family members being gone, extreme persecution, the rise of the antichrist, and evil beyond measure. They either experience regret and finally desire Jesus for themselves or embrace evil, because at that point there's no in-between.

The movie scarred me to the point that I actually had a nightmare of the rapture happening. I was stuck in the church basement, unable to find my best friend. When the nightmare ended, I felt my way out of my bedroom and whimpered through the dark until I reached my mother's bedside to tell her about it. I'm pretty sure I had accepted Christ into my heart prior to the dream, but all I know is little Tarah had to *double*-check and get "re-saved" for good measure that night!

And then there was one hurricane season when I blasted Kirk Franklin's *Hello Fear* album from my computer, singing the lyrics aloud and trying to find peace as I readied myself for Christ's return . . . just in case. I'd look out of the window to see if the sky was cracking with chariots coming through! I wasn't excited awaiting His return. To be honest, even now, I'm just like, "Uh, Jesus? Can ya, like, hold on just a sec?" I want to get married and have kids and look back on life! (You can't tell me I'm alone on that part!)

At the time of that album, people (many believers and unbelievers alike) kept mentioning that the year 2012 would be the end of the world. I knew Matthew 24:36: "However, no one knows the day or hour when these things will happen, not even the angels in heaven or the Son himself. Only the Father knows." But when I looked at the news and saw wars, rumors of wars, natural disasters, and beyond, I was like, well, look at the signs . . . even if He doesn't return in 2012, it must be soon!

And then there were the few times I woke up from naps in a frenzy, recognized that I was still alive, and repented and apologized to God as if He was going to change His mind about me. I remember waking up in the middle of the night to a dry voice filled with doom on a Christian radio station or chords to a song that started out so eerily that I fought sleep and looked for the sunrise. These things didn't happen often, but they were enough to leave an impression on me.

Oh, and it *definitely* didn't help that there were many evils being exposed in Hollywood around the year 2012 either. I was terrified because I felt darkness sweeping over the world at an incessant pace. I was not and am still not into conspiracies, but I could discern between the parts that are far-fetched and the truth. It was enough to convince me to delete certain artists off my phone, cry over those who were lost, or be in a state of shock about those who blatantly disrespected God through their lyrics and performances.

Despite all this fear, I knew God's love to be true not only through biblical stories but through witnessing my mother's daily suffering right before my eyes. I saw how God showered love on my mom in and out of emergency rooms, strokes, surgeries, and whatever the enemy tried to use to break her. I considered that love as enough . . . because she had it.

I'm not too sure when I received it for myself, but I do know that church choir practices during my high school years got me closer to Him. The lyrics of the songs we sang made me begin to experience His goodness in a new way. And even though the motivation I had at first was fear, I was learning on my own . . . reading the Word, understanding it, and applying it to my life. In college, I joined the gospel choir, met a good friend, and we attended an amazing church that aided in our spiritual growth, totally transforming our ways of thinking. And of course I'm blessed to have had people to admire while I was growing up.

As I matured, I began to desire to serve God more and more. There was one notable moment post–college graduation when I was hit with God's overwhelming love, but it wasn't until a few years later that I realized I lived most of my life with a distorted view of God.

So what changed? My heart, my mind, my eyes.

I asked God to change my perception. My surface love for God grew into something deeper when He led me into situations where it was just me and Him, and I needed His love to pick me up. I couldn't run to my mother with all of my issues; I had to look to Him. He wanted the chance to be my best friend and the Father who embraces me.

The Distorted Mirror

I used to feel like I didn't have a salvation story; I considered my mother's testimony as my own. In fact, "Her story is mine" is what I used to say for years. Until I realized it wasn't. Or rather, that it wasn't my entire story.

One day in the summer of 2020, I had the idea to produce a confidence series primarily on my YouTube channel, Adorned in Armor. Inspired by *Claim Your Crown*, I called the playlist "Kingdom Confidence." I was having a great creative session, jotting down subtopics to cover, and the ideas flowed freely until I suddenly stopped. I realized there was no way I could go forward without starting from the very beginning.

Accepting Christ as our Lord and Savior is the initial step into our royal inheritances and the kingdom key we need to rule our minds and wisely navigate our emotions, fears, and triggers. **I fully believe that in order to flourish and tap into unshakeable confidence and worth, we must first redefine who we are through the eyes of our Father. And we can't do that if we have the wrong view of Him.** It's through getting to know Him that we, in turn, get to know ourselves and the purpose we're called to live out. I am confident in Christ because of the full assurance I have of who I am in Him, who He is, and where He is taking me. I desire for you to feel the same.

I knew I had to share my salvation story with my subscribers online. It's a testimony I wasn't aware I had until I considered how my relationship with Christ now flows from a place of love: a father-daughter relationship. It dawned on me that my testimony is that I now desire to please my King, *period*. Not because I'm scared but because I want to grow and fall in deeper awe of Him, day after day. **Fear imprisoned me, forcing me to turn to religion, but now love freely joins me to Christ.** Overcoming fear-based faith is my personal testimony. I love the Lord not because I was taught to: I love the Lord because I have tasted and seen for *myself* that He is good.

As I was about to hit Publish on the testimony video, an overwhelming hesitation came upon me and I froze . . . but then I thought, "There's absolutely *no* way I went through all that work of filming and editing for me not to share it with the world!" That, and God reminded me that He gave me this message for a reason. Thousands of views and hundreds of comments later, I discovered why: the second coming is a secret fear many believers are struggling with! I had commenters as young as thirteen years of age and as seasoned as sixty years of age sharing how much my confession and testimony freed them. I prayed that my testimony would demonstrate how it is possible to choose God out of sincerity, to have a heart after His so intently that you can't imagine life or eternity without Him. I shared those words to show that it is possible to get to this place. To the one who desires God but is fearful of what His return looks like, I am ministering to you. I posted the video to minister to those who love God but desire to love Him *more* and look forward to His coming . . . and it spoke volumes!

But I also received comments, direct messages, and private emails from people who are paralyzed and paranoid due to this fear. They are Christians who have never confessed this to anyone and feel foolish writing it out, believers who can't get out of bed due to anxiety and hopelessness, children of God who are crying uncontrollably every day. They are followers of Christ who feel they need to get saved "multiple times," who want to hope in God's love for them but can't, who have lost their fire for God, who have begged Him for an innate hunger of His Word and to work on them as He needs but haven't felt the change. They are at a loss for what to do. They feel like "sitting ducks," yet are alert at all times as they study the Ten Commandments "in proper order." They believe God can do great things—including free them from their fears—but are heartbroken to think of God leaving them behind on earth, abandoning them.

One woman told me she "tries so hard," that she constantly cries out and begs God "to recognize [her] as His daughter."

It pained me to hear all that; the feedback opened my eyes to how broken the body of Christ is. Maybe you don't struggle with this particular fear, but everyone struggles with something. At one point or another, we have all fallen victim to the enemy's schemes of distorting the image of God. And his goal is the same for all of us.

You see, your enemy, Satan, doesn't want you to realize who you are. He does not want you to live out your purpose, and he definitely doesn't want you experiencing the love of God here on earth or in heaven. **Satan will try to use anything—yes, especially faith that is built on the wrong foundation—to wipe you out.**

Satan doesn't want you to understand that you are saved by grace through faith.[1] He wants you to focus on good works, duties, and the distractions of this world. He doesn't want you to cast your cares on God.[2] He wants you to sleep with your fears, to coddle them, to feed them in your heart and surrender to them in the battlefield of your mind.

The devil is called the father of lies, so anything that he suggests (yes, even in the form of your thoughts) is the farthest thing from the truth.[3] If he tells you, "God doesn't really love you" or "Jesus didn't accept you" or "You'll never get through this," believe the very opposite. Satan will always present you with "false evidence appearing real" or what we also know as fear. But thank God, the truth of who our Lord and Savior is supersedes all that.

Fear Is Not God's Language

Among the comments on my video was one that struck me in a different way: someone commented that what I was teaching was not biblical. This person argued that without fearing God, we will never change our attitude toward sin because we don't fear the consequences.

The commenter addressed me using the analogy of a doctor: a physician must use fear tactics to convince their patient they're in danger. The cure means nothing to the patient if the patient isn't afraid of their condition. In other words, people won't see the necessity of Christ if they aren't shown the seriousness of sin, which includes the reality of hell. The commenter argued that fear is the only key to convincing the sinner they're in terrible danger.

In some ways, I agree. Sin *is* serious. Hell is real. And yes, we are at the mercy of God. But ultimately, the commenter's view doesn't align with the character of God. When sharing the Good News of Jesus Christ, it is pivotal to include who God truly is (inherently good) and who we are in His perfect and righteous sight (His beloved). What we say has to encompass the reason we are in this fallen state and what Jesus suffered on the cross in the place of us sinners. It must contain the call to salvation (a one-time occurrence) and repentance, which is a lifelong journey of honoring God's will over ours. But fear should not be the motivating force.

To reiterate: what I am *not* doing is telling you that the all-encompassing God is solely about love and acceptance. What I am saying is, we can go deeper. **Fear-based faith is not a true relationship; God wants your heart.** First John

4:18 tells us, "There is no fear in love. But perfect love drives out fear, because fear has to do with punishment. The one who fears is not made perfect in love."[4] The Bible tells us that perfect love *casts out* all fear. Remember, I went from being someone who was fearful of punishment to someone who serves God because of the desire of wanting to love Him more and more. So if you're struggling with this, it is okay to *ask* God to give you the desire for more of Him.

There's a difference between fearing God out of reverence and fearing God out of the belief He is gleefully waiting to shoot us down to hell with one wrong move. (I'll be speaking more about what fearing God is *supposed* to look like later.) While it's important to take the day of judgment seriously, it's also crucial for the believer to have confidence that God will accept them when living lives of repentance. As we embrace His love, it's also pivotal that we do not take advantage of His mercy by purposely breaking His heart because we know He will take us back. He desires true relationship—one where love is given and received with an honest and repentant heart.

I like how John Piper describes this: "According to 1 John 4:17–18, there is a way to approach the day of judgment with fearless confidence. No one who is willing to follow Christ needs to be frightened at the approach of death. None of us who accepts this teaching will have to approach the judgment seat of God with our fingers crossed, wondering if we are going to make it."[5]

Good stuff, huh? Let me tell you how I responded to the negative comment on my video. I shared how the value of Christ is not dependent on whether we see it. He is good.

He is love. And He desires that we see and know His heart. I don't know of any doctor who uses fear tactics for a patient to understand the side effects of medication or the reality of disease. I know doctors who use truth. Our physician in heaven does this while also relaying warnings. Sometimes the truth will hurt, but God did not call us to live our lives in fear when we pick up our crosses and follow Him.

I share this all with you to say . . . fear tactics and threats aren't how God works. Romans 2:4 tells us that it is God's *kindness* that leads us to repentance. We should not be presenting faith in Christ as a simple way to escape eternal torment away from Him. We can't scare anyone into loving Him. Frantic and fearful prayers aren't what faith is about. Christ wants to free people from death because of His great love.

Many people have the perception of God not being good or merciful, so think about it: who would want to get to know a God who allows calamity and seems gleeful about consigning them to an eternity of fear and torment? His love, His sacrifice, and His Word are enough to draw them out of fear and into relationship.

As I was writing this chapter, I came across an enlightening article that captured my exact sentiments. It read:

> I believe the words and life of Christ are worth emulating and that His ways are worth walking in, but I refuse to cajole someone into doing so because they're terrified of Hell. When it comes to relationships with people, real love is never grounded in fear. It is never chosen to avoid damage. It never comes packaged as a threat. We would

never look at such things between two people and call it love—we would call it coercion.

And if God is as loving and good as we claim, love for God cannot be born out of this kind of fear either.

What Jesus offers is beautiful. . . . Let's try living in such a way that faith is something they choose with joy because their hearts are touched and they are moved to reciprocate with the giver. This is how love works.

It is a dream, not a nightmare.[6]

I resonated with that deeply . . . and I know where the writer was going, but I'd rather say God's love is real life. A "royal reality" is what I call it. And it's yours for the taking.

The Power to Overcome

I've had people tell me they couldn't become Christians because they could never be "good enough." But perfection isn't expected of you.

You do *not* have to be perfect to accept Christ into your heart.

You don't have to be perfect even after.

In fact, there's no such thing as a perfect Christian. None of us would have the ability to stand in the presence of the Holy God without redemption. It is the Lord who redeems us and draws us nearer to Him. Even if you carelessly chose disobedience and are now afraid because of it, God is waiting with open arms.

Romans 10:9 says, "If you confess with your mouth, 'Jesus is Lord,' and believe in your heart that God raised Him from the dead, you will be saved."[7] This is an immediate exchange and a lifelong adventure. And if you truly seek God, you will find that He will do a work in you.

If you accepted Christ as your personal Savior, you are saved, *period*. Your home is in heaven! When we give our lives to Him, we gain forever. Sin has serious repercussions, but we don't have to fear God's wrath when we cultivate a heart that desires to honor Him. Sometimes that desire doesn't come instantaneously, but you can receive God's love right now. You don't have to live afraid. The point of following Christ is discovering true freedom that can be found in Him alone. Don't allow Satan, another person, or even you yourself to keep you in bondage. Begin with asking God to give you a heart that desires to know Him and love Him more.

For many, it is hell that captures their attention, then they discover who Christ really is, and His character takes center stage in their lives. But there are also those whose minds are filled with the fear of hell so they attempt to work their way to heaven and never experience the heart of God. You, my friend, don't have to live like that. You don't have to prove a thing. You don't have to strive to "be good" in order to obtain a home your Father has already promised you.

Sometimes, we just don't know how to accept a gift that's invaluable. A present that's priceless and keeps giving even after it's gifted can be a hard concept to grasp, let alone receive. But please find peace in knowing there's nothing and no way we can pay God back except to live our lives as an offering unto Him—struggles and all. John 1:12 says, "Yet to all who did receive him, to those who believed in his name, he gave the right to become children of God."[8] Receive this gift, queen! It has your name engraved on it. You are a daughter of the Most High King.

You don't have to be afraid of the judgment day to discover whether your relationship with Christ was founded on a false perception of His character. One thing I've noticed among the community of believers is how we are hyperaware that God is Jehovah-Shafat, or Jehovah our Judge, but we often fail to realize that He rules and reigns in *our favor*. We see crystal clear in regard to how He will not leave the guilty unpunished, but our sight gets foggy when it comes to realizing He is our judge who will protect our rights before all. Isaiah 33:22 says, "For the LORD is our judge, our lawgiver, and our king. He will care for us and save us."

The government is unchanging in the kingdom of God, therefore the laws He has established will never change. If we remain dedicated to His decrees, then the promise of His rescue will be manifested in us. It's a verdict that cannot change, either!

Furthermore, the crowned Prince of Peace, Jesus Christ—the ultimate sacrifice—is our lawyer. We are no longer separated from the Lawgiver, God, because His Son's resurrection power made it possible for Him to intercede for us, fighting our case in court and giving us the power to overcome sin, traumas, fears, worries, and our thoughts.

Because of Jesus's sacrifice, we need not be cautious about approaching our Father. Hebrews 4:16 says, "So we should come near to God and we should not be afraid. God is our King. We can ask him to help us when we need help. We know that he will forgive us and he will be kind to us in whatever way we need."[9] In other words, obsessively trying to fix ourselves won't work. Instead, may we invite God in and allow the gift of the Holy Spirit to work through us.

We've been looking at the wrong picture, but now that we can see more clearly, disrupting fear and drawing a true picture of God via intimacy is the goal. May we dwell in His presence, praise Him for who He is, and pray with confidence that He will free us from strongholds in His perfect timing.

Reflection Questions

I have a few questions at the end of each chapter in this book that I think would be great for you as a journaling prompt. They're pretty . . . intimate. My favorite way to journal is putting pen to paper, but making notes on your phone comes in handy, too! Choose what works best for you, and get ready to reflect on and respond to these questions.

1. How do you see God?
2. How do you believe He sees you?
3. I shared with you how the fear of the second coming was a scar in my relationship with Jesus. Is there a fear in your friendship with Christ that you need Him to heal? If so, what is it?

I pray my testimony encourages you, reassures you, and changes your view of God's goodness, love, and relentless pursuit of you. You can watch the full video on YouTube: Adorned in Armor, or you can scan the code on your mobile device below!

2

Imposter

Dissatisfaction and Disrupting a View of Self

My flesh and my heart may fail,
but God is the strength of my heart
and my portion forever.

Psalm 73:26 NIV

I have something else to confess, and I hope you're not judgey (hey, I'll still love ya). Alright, here goes: the idea of heaven freaks me out. I mean, not all the time, but yeah, sometimes it does. I opened up about overcoming my fear of the second coming, but this one . . . this is an ongoing whammy that's way scarier and pops its head a few times a year.

I'm aware of how weird that may sound to you. Maybe you're thinking, *Uh, excuse me,* Christian *author, how can you be a believer writing these books and you're afraid of the very place you're to look forward to living out your eternity?* I've had the same thoughts.

I struggled with thinking something was wrong with me for the longest time because of this "heaven phobia." I recognize the fruit of the Spirit in myself, I love my ever-growing personal relationship with Christ, and everything I do is to please my Father and bring the honor due His name. But I have wondered, Why am I not like the other Christians who are so excited about Christ's coming? The enemy has dared to launch missiles of imposter syndrome against me ever since.

To be clear: I'm not talking about a fear of the rapture and the judgment that I was referring to earlier—I've conquered that. Nor is this a fear of death. I'm not worried about where I am going to go. I know that whenever God closes this earthly chapter, I'll enter into heaven and will be adorned with the crown of life. But the idea of heaven doesn't necessarily give me peace . . . at least, not always.

I have this memory of returning from college and attending a service at my old church. That Sunday, a young woman sang "I Will Rise" by Chris Tomlin. While it was a beautiful song meant to comfort and empower, the lyrics actually terrified me at the time. My reaction was similar to the few times when I would find myself thinking of eternity before going to bed and suddenly begin gasping for air, immediately immersed in a blanket of thick nothingness where I couldn't breathe.

After the sermon, my pastor welcomed congregants up for prayer, salvation, or rededication. I waited until after church was over and walked up to the altar as tears streamed down my face. My pastor wondered why my face was downcast; he tried to cheer me up by saying my rededication to Christ was cause for celebration. But really, I was in mourning, and I was trapped in it. Surely, no one would understand. It didn't make sense to open up to a nonbeliever about it, and as my pastor demonstrated, other Christians wouldn't understand the heaviness that weighed down on my heart.

But I'll try my best to explain it to you. As a goal- and results-driven individual, one thing I'm drawn to is how there's always a "next" in our everyday. Not only that but there is always a high honor to obtain in each level that is reached. It keeps life interesting! I quickly understood that I don't need to be the best, but at all times I would like to perform my best. I'm all about excellence, and no, that isn't a bad thing. It is never about the accolades either, as I rapidly realized that none satisfied me. It is the adventure and the idea that "there is more" that is so appealing.

From elementary to graduate school, I was the student who would do the extra credit assignment in order to obtain the highest score. I enjoy the idea of excelling in industries of interest and standing out there. Society taught us that once we get through elementary, middle, and high school, we must prepare for college. Next is graduate school, and maybe additional years for a doctorate if need be. Then there's building a career, marriage, and children, and in between are many surprises, twists, turns, and trials that are ultimately working for our good. For me, it's like, "Okay, we experience all that and then we get to heaven and . . . that's it?" That's *the end*?

My Spirit versus My Mind

I have a desire for more, and this desire was especially visible in the seasons when I was bored with life and expressed that to God. Newness is refreshing for me. I remember the revelation that came to me when I first read Ecclesiastes 3:11: "Yet God has made everything beautiful for its own time. He has planted eternity in the human heart, but even so, people cannot see the whole scope of God's work from beginning to end."

We often feel like strangers in this world and still desire to play a part in "forever." We have the desire for our legacies to matter and to understand why we are here. We can't make sense of it all on this side of heaven because God planted eternity in our hearts so that in our confusion and yearning, we will make the Lord our quest. Writer Mary Fairchild says it like this: "Even still, once we find him and know that he is the answer to all of our questions, many of the endless mysteries of God continue to remain unanswered. . . . We learn to trust that God has obscured certain secret things from us for a reason. But we can also trust that his reason is beautiful in its time."[1]

Ecclesiastes 3:11 gave me relief as I learned we were designed this way on purpose. The "God-shaped hole" concept reveals that we all have a void within us that can be filled solely by God.[2] It is the intrinsic yearning of the human heart for something bigger than ourselves, something otherworldly. God made humanity for His eternal purpose, and only God can fulfill our desire for eternity.

It's not uncommon for humankind to either disregard that longing or attempt to quench it with fillers: careers, education, family, money, success—anything other than God. Romans 1:18–22 makes it plain how humanity disregards the very attributes God makes known to us. Instead, we're prone to taking up idols in His place. And in chasing things that are temporary, we stay unfulfilled and then we get pensive, beating up ourselves because we can be happy for only some time.

In the Bible, King Solomon had it all—wisdom, riches, looks, fame, and wives out the wazoo. And yet, he exemplified how none of what he possessed came close to quenching his thirst for eternity. He proclaimed it all "vanity" because those things did not satisfy.[3] (Reading Ecclesiastes used to be so depressing for me; I thought, *Truly, what's the point of* any *of this?!*)

Here's the thing: attempting to fill the void with anything other than God is not my problem, or rather, it is not the underlying root of my fear. All I desire is to be filled with God! And I have full understanding that nothing in this world will ever satisfy me. So why am I concerned that an eternity with God won't either?

I used to struggle with thinking, *Hmm, maybe something went wrong with me.* But I dismissed the lie, knowing that couldn't be it, because God does not make mistakes! Every move is calculated, every brush stroke He makes is intentional. So the enemy suggested, *Maybe it's just you.* And I began to think maybe there's a malfunction in my mind . . . an issue that I brought upon myself. Because I can't wrap my mind around truly believing that once I get to heaven I will feel it in my bones every single day that "Yes, this is it." This is what my soul was longing for. I hope that happens. I want to believe it fully.

No, I don't *enjoy* the suffering here on earth. But I do enjoy the moments I have with my family; I savor their company. No, I don't adopt the patterns of this world nor do I love my life until death. But I *do* like how there is always a next, always something to look forward to. I recently entered my late twenties, and when that fear of feeling suffocated in heaven showed its ugly head one night, I thought to myself, *Ya know what, I'm just gonna deal.* I mean, we're all going to pass on anyway! (In case you haven't noticed by now, I'm rather matter-of-fact—especially with myself!)

I fully embrace the fact that my spirit yearns for heaven (and that part gives me peace)—but my mind sometimes struggles with reconciling the idea that I will have so much life to look forward to while I'm there. (Reasoning is a silent killer, indeed.) While I struggle with this occasional apprehensiveness, I understand and revere the Word of God as truth. So I figure it won't be until I get to heaven that I realize my hesitations were for naught. I look forward to being proved wrong!

Reflection Questions

1. Have you ever disqualified yourself from the gifts of God because you believed the lie that something was wrong with you?
2. Do you ever struggle with feeling like an "imposter" as a Christian? If so, what triggers that feeling?
3. What fear are you afraid to share with another believer? What is holding you back?

3

The Mute Button

A Healthy Desire for More vs. Discontentment

The LORD will fight for you; you need only to be still.

Exodus 14:14 NIV

Disclaimer: this is not a book about doom and gloom! I repeat, this is not a book about doom and gloom. And yes, I'm talking to you in the back, too! I want to emphasize that all our fears and worries have a birthplace. They can be born *years* ago and in private; Satan nurtures them in a bed of lies. These babies grow up and manifest differently, and oftentimes, it's not until trauma strikes or God reveals them to you personally that you can begin to address them and heal.

The enemy likes to get you early in life. He isolates you in your thoughts; he makes you feel as if there's something wrong with you that cannot be fixed. But life is a journey of constant discovery and recovery. One of my own personal discoveries is God revealing how my other worries (like the fear of being dissatisfied with life) ultimately stem from this anxiousness about heaven. You'll soon see how.

Since that disclaimer is out of the way . . . quick question! Have you ever played Would You Rather? As a child, two options played in my mind: Would I rather *burn* for eternity or be *bored* for an eternity? I chose the latter. Now, while I'm not bouncing off the walls, waiting in eager expectation for heaven at this present moment, I do understand we won't be doing the same thing over and over and there *will* be ultimate fulfillment, praise the good Lord.

But still, sameness scares me. And the enemy plays on it . . . especially in the seasons when he makes me feel like I am doing nothing. A recent example was the world's initial lockdown due to COVID-19. A few years prior, I stopped contributing to *Teen Vogue* and the *Haitian Times* because God showed me that it was a season when He wanted me to focus on all the ideas that He had given me for my brand. I worked on my fashion-and-faith business, traveled often for speaking engagements, and suddenly signed a three-book deal. I released the first of those books right before the COVID lockdown.

But when the pandemic hit, I found it difficult to create for months. Thankfully, the deadline for my second book was pushed back so I didn't have to focus on writing. But it took great effort to do anything else. I was a bit stir-crazy. I'd already been working from home before the pandemic began, but the loss of my creative energy made me feel like I simply wasn't living. Who was I now?

Brain Overload

My thoughts ran rampant, reminding me how bored and unfulfilled I felt. I was frustrated, hurt, and confused. I considered how much pain my mother is in. I remembered her avoidable stroke, unsuccessful surgeries, bladder issues, and the ever-growing list of new ailments. Will the chronic pain she has suffered through the past twenty-one years ever end? I fought worry while she was in grave condition in the hospital, fighting COVID. And when she made it back home, my thoughts kept me up at night searching for solutions that would keep her from falling if she fell asleep while standing (due to extreme fatigue and prescribed muscle relaxers to help relieve her pain). These ruminations kept me up until four in the morning while I monitored her movements through FaceTime as I worked. I figured that was better than the many times I would abruptly wake up after hearing a loud thump and jump out of bed, run upstairs, and check on her.

I fretted over the fact that I was twenty-five and living in my parents' house (that's not unheard of in Haitian culture, and I actually *love* being here). But I was not bringing in enough income to help my family in the way I wished. The book advances I received went only so far. And social media was one of my primary sources of revenue, but with the pandemic, that came to a complete halt.

My mind told me there was no point in showing up there. Social media, I mean. I felt I no longer had anything to say, and then I struggled with discouragement. When I rebuked the enemy and pushed past that pessimism to post something, my thoughts told me I should be embarrassed by the lack of engagement I received online.

I know the lack of engagement was a mixture of causes. Factor one: the algorithms of social media platforms are built to champion the work of white content creators—it's proven. Creators of color have long acknowledged that social algorithms of these popular platforms like Instagram and TikTok were constructed with white people in mind. I can take you down a rabbit hole sharing the very personal experiences of my peers or go into detail with an extensive list of resources that go deeper in the discussions of how less discoverable and credited Black creators are on social media,[1] the time when social media decided to give a boost to Black creators in the height of police brutality,[2] or the very obvious racial pay gap between white and BIPOC in influencer marketing.[3] Instead, I'll share this quote from Adam Mosseri, the head of Instagram itself, who made an announcement about how Instagram will do better to stop limiting the reach of Black creators and will work on fixing Instagram's "algorithmic bias" influenced by the "underlying systems" they've created—and that it'll take time.[4]

Factor two: though I know it messes with my visibility, it's best for my mental health to post primarily when I feel like God is leading me to, or if there's a sponsored collaboration, or honestly, when I get dolled up and have pictures to share.

Factor three: I'm blatantly made aware of those who see my content and scroll past or they send or save in private. Thank you, Instagram Analytics . . . oh, and I can't forget about you, Story Views!

You know what they say about how there's more people watching you in silence than you think? Yeah, that's cute and all, but during the pandemic, I wondered why God was allowing my community to take so long to find me. I would compare stats with those in my field, and it was simply not adding up. I started my brand to lead people to live fashionable, purpose-filled lives, and it brought about many amazing paid opportunities that allowed me to serve others. I barely understand the numbers, but I do know if they're interfering with the ways in which I can flow in my creativity (sometimes, I wonder what's the point of publishing if it's not being seen) and provide for my family, then, yeah, we have a problem.

I look forward to the day I don't have to look at my statistics as a one-woman team; my staff will give me quarterly reports. The reason I occasionally check them is because it's necessary to determine what works across my platforms and what doesn't. I have never and will never be into metrics, but social media is one of my jobs, so yes, it matters. Not only that, those metrics are a point of reference for my publisher or any promising outlet that is interested in my brand.

Putting your all into everything and not seeing anything for it does affect you on an emotional level, too. I just couldn't understand why my work was not being recognized. On one night, I wrote to God, saying:

I don't go chasing trends and though I've been feeling left out, especially in the fashion field, I'm not chasing opportunities. As I said last year, Lord, only You make me relevant. I have to put on my armor in a new way. Help me,

Lord. Proverbs 13:12 says "hope deferred makes the heart sick" and Lord, I've been sick. I've been beaten down and hurt and in pieces. I've been crying yet always showing up, misunderstood, overlooked, persecuted and suffering for so long. My best friend and family honor Your process with me but they confessed they thought I was set for life in college. Yet, here I am. My hope is there but it's weak. I've been patient, Lord. . . . I've been embarrassed and looked down upon. I've been made a fool. . . . The end of the proverb says, "but a longing fulfilled is a tree of life." Father, please, heal my heart, breathe new life.

Reeling from My Relationships

Have you ever casually scrolled through social media only to see a post that stopped you in your tracks? Maybe you caught a subtweet or came across someone from your past who hurt you. That moment can be heavy, can't it? As I was dealing with the social engagement stuff, my social feed was also amplifying the posts of old friends who betrayed or used me. Seeing the posts illustrated how they were either seemingly doing better or they did not have to deal with the consequences of their actions—or both. I was the one hurting. They were shining and I was in the dark. I felt rejected when I realized I was ghosted after I'd been used. I was confused when my accomplishments were met with jealousy and resentment. I felt stupid when I reached out to see if there was anything I did wrong on my end and in each circumstance was told, "Nothing, we're good!"

This feeling is something I'm familiar with. I grew up in proximity to someone I felt could never truly be happy for me, and I was also in a huge church community where it seemed most girls (emphasis on "most"—not all) chose to see me in the lens of haughtiness. I was accustomed to that—the spreading of rumors, the side-eyeing, the copying . . . It was normal, living like that. From my teenage years to adulthood, I was indifferent. I had the attitude of, if they want to talk, let me give them the reason to! I had a great group of friends and a sister who would go to bat for me, but if I needed to, I was always confident to stand on my own. My confidence was a shield for me.

In the last three years, the lack of receptiveness bothered me at times because I felt I was robbed of the opportunity to show who I was. I didn't crave friendship, but for goodness' sake, what is wrong with being *kind*? There were a few times when someone would say to me or of me, "You're so much nicer than I thought." Ultimately, however, I had to come to the realization that people will choose to see me in the way *they* want regardless of having the accurate picture.

God revealed and healed the traumas that came with growing up with a brave face—one of them being no longer feeling the need to tone down my accomplishments in order for a friend to feel special and recognized. It's a process, though; I'm still learning to undo what became a habit and to hype myself up for every milestone.

The hit of betrayal and/or jealousy is different, however, when those you've *allowed* into your life are the ones who use, abuse, and leave. To be betrayed by people who have access to your personal space . . . oof, I never related more to the story of Joseph! When you build real relationships with women who see you and honor God, it's so much more of a shock when sin gets in the way. You almost feel as if because we are believers on fire for Christ, there's no way there could be room for messiness. What I also couldn't get my mind around was how this could happen to me as one who champions women so fiercely. My heart is so loud with my praise of others that it genuinely was a form of culture shock when someone chose bitterness. But then I learned that we will experience the most persecution and rejection in regard to the community God calls us to. Still, that doesn't take away the sting of the hurt.

I love freely and use wisdom in how I extend myself. I don't give everyone access to all of me. My circle is small, and I can easily distinguish which queen is in what court. I guard my heart, I use discernment, I judge character well. But I ain't Jesus, so while I may know some relationships are seasonal, I am not privy to knowing all of the details. I'm kind, but when necessary, I'm good for a cutoff. Moving on is my forte. But I also honor what the Word says and will exercise due diligence to part amicably, even if the other party doesn't want to embrace the truth of their feelings.[5]

Trusting God with My Heart

One thing I always say is that we are all in our own lanes; there is no need to compete or compare, so I'm open to celebrating anyone who is in my life or not. But what I'm *not* okay with is the maltreatment or mishandling of people and getting away with it. I felt God allowed that a lot when it came to me. So, during lockdown, I got upset that I honored God so much that I still chose to be the bigger person, and yet I suffered. I was hurt because I felt like God let others get away with how I was harmed. In fact, my mind tried to convince me that He liked it. I told Him, "You told me that You would fight for me but You're not." I did all I could to protect myself, but it felt like He wasn't doing His part in protecting me. It was a battle of thoughts, having to constantly remind myself of the truth and how I need only to be still.

At the time, I was reading the book of Genesis and came across verse 3 of chapter 12, where God promises Abraham that He will curse those who dishonor him. As a spiritual descendant of Abraham, I rose up and said, "Do it, Jesus! Have your way." I was all for it, pitchfork in hand, smile on my face, and hurt in my heart.

I recognized new triggers: Coming across Christian influencers who used and ghosted me, and watching them blossom beautifully in metrics. Seeing my peers or prominent figures in Christian influencing or podcasting view my message but not reply. Discovering those plagiarizing chapters of *Claim Your Crown* and creating events around them without even so much as a nod to the source. For the sake of my well-being, I began to mute them on social media. Proactive in nature, I refused to believe that somehow that "evidence" proved God wasn't fighting for me.

When it comes to opening my heart to the point of vulnerability for the sake of someone else's advancement, I have to consciously enlist God's help. This type of intimate exposure of self can be really risky, scary even.

Have you been hurt to the point where the wound has either made you close off or you're able to let people in, but warily? I had to go through a whole process of praying for my enemies, continuously asking the Lord to help me heal and still maintain my heart for women and for the strength to root for people He had previously placed in my life. I prayed that He would help me not to take things personally, and I asked for more patience to continue to wait for my own breakthrough—whether it be for my business, ministry, personal brand, or family.

I've asked the Lord to remove from my memory the list of wrongs committed against me. Of course, my heart hasn't completely forgotten, but I have overcome a lot. Just know, words can't express the hurt I felt not only in those previous friendships but in my love life, too. What took my breath away wasn't how it all piled up . . . What broke my heart was really how, in those moments, it felt like God betrayed me, too.

A Healthy Desire for More

In the wilderness of my thoughts during the pandemic, there was one moment where God showed me why I was seeing "the ugly stuff." I was seeing those things because He was revealing them to me. This changed everything for me. I was reminded that as much as we think we know ourselves, we all have ugly stuff within us. And though it felt like a self-discovery, it was actually a God-discovery, because God is within me. God was revealing the ugly stuff to me so that I became aware of what He desires to uproot. He is not disgusted or repulsed when He finds ungodliness within us; the Lord alone can do a beautification in us.

I wouldn't have realized this had I not been willing to seek a quiet place in all of the noise. When I was scared of what was within me and when I didn't understand why it was there, I ran to my Creator. You'll notice this one constant about me: I will always go to my Father and share my heart.

Oftentimes, I go to God requesting more of His presence, more of His revelation, more of His love, more of His promises. I'm no David, but I always wondered why Psalm 34:8 says, "Taste and see that the LORD is good." I don't want just a taste; why can't I drink in full? Why can't we fill ourselves with the Living Water and topple over?!

God has *so* many layers. And I genuinely enjoy going deeper and uncovering all that I can. I can speak and write about His love because I know it is there. I've seen it with my own eyes, felt it in my heart, and bowed down in awe of it. I wish I could feel it all the time or be more aware of it. Like many believers, I have tasted joy but I have not experienced the fullness of it.

However, I fully embrace the process of getting there. It's healthy to ask for more, especially when approaching the throne of the One who knows and will give what's best in His time. *And*, it is indeed possible to be content and still desire more for yourself in a way that pleases God. I am a huge dreamer and have been waiting for many things to come to pass. Much of this crazy faith comes from how I believe in so much for myself (and that's not a bad thing).

As believers, we are not meant to live boring or ordinary lives. As heirs of the kingdom, we inherit immeasurably more—all that we can ask for or think. Since I strongly believe God has so much in store for us, it's long been a pleasure of mine to push anyone who crosses my path to live purposefully and to believe bigger! It sincerely brings me so much joy encouraging you into victory. I understand it can feel like it's taking forever to get there, so we need all the encouragement we can get.

I'm not much of a complainer; I believe it's a waste of time. If I can do something to change my situation, I will. If God tells me to wait, then I will. And I am devoted to waiting well. But honey, waiting is not for the weak! I often feel the weight and can totally relate to letting everything out before the Lord because it feels like you can't hold on any longer. One night, at 3:17 a.m., I wrote:

> God, all of my efforts feel futile. People are posting fluff and being recognized. I've been suffering for so long when my platforms are dedicated to You. My website, podcasts, Instagram . . . I'm so grateful You gave them all to me, Lord. I'm grateful with where You have brought me. But God, I am not making enough to support myself the way I would like. I'm grateful to be in my parents' house but I can't help them the way I want. I do the research, did the schooling and internships. I check my heart, I go to You. I'm not crying because I don't believe You won't take me out; I'm crying because I'm still here.

In preparation for this book, I reread my 2020 journal and teared up when I read certain entries; the one I just shared was one of them. It's these lines for me: "I check my heart, I go to You. I'm not crying because I don't believe You won't take me out; I'm crying because *I'm still here.*"

You see, my word of the year for 2020 was "yes" as a reminder of my dedication to obey God no matter what that looked like. That year, I did literally everything in my power to set myself up for success. I put Christ at the forefront, especially with my work, even though I honestly was fed up with everything and (almost) everyone. Yet, God required me to show up, and I did in crazy ways for my business, audience, and ultimately, His glory.

I did the work behind the scenes because though work is hard for me, I also find it enjoyable. I worked overtime because I was doing what I felt I needed to do. It is not only my nature but I showed up for work in order to continue to build the strong foundation for the long run. I was running too hard with no financial stability or honor for so long. Too long. At the end of 2020, I declared that the following year would be the year I would actually see something for my work. The year I would begin to reap, the year I would see my inheritance.

As I finish writing this book, *I'm still here* in a lot of ways. I'm still here, surrendered to God. I'm still here, standing formidably because of His grace. I'm still here, even when my circumstances aren't much different. I still have many private battles, but I fight disillusionment with gratitude.

Gratitude is a state of mind we must hold on to, and we must cling to it like it's all we've got. Sometimes, gratitude looks like a weeping session of worship. Other times, it can look like full, unadulterated happiness. And then there are the times when gratitude looks like an honest conversation. I once told God, "I always listen to Your instruction, but I don't feel like You're appreciative of me."

The audacity, eh? I know, you're probably thinking how is *that* an expression of gratitude? It's a moment of gratefulness for me because I fully embrace that God wants to hear all of my hurts. I'm grateful that I don't have to hold back when expressing myself to my Father. I don't have to do anything; I can freely just be. And He wants your all, too, even the raw, honest feelings *and* the ugly stuff. A good Father always desires to know how their child is hurting, who did it, why it happened. And even if we can't see it on our side, our Good Father is already working on ways to kiss the wound and make it all better.

The tears I wept on that night of my confession to Him didn't compare to the ones where my eyes were too blurred for me to see which lines to write on. But no matter what I was feeling, no matter what I expressed, I made sure I went to bed with a thanks on my lips. Even if I choked and couldn't sing His praises, I could whisper or I could write it down: blessed be the name of the Lord.

The Ugliness of Discontentment

Let's rewind for a bit. I'd like to address something quickly before moving forward: just as there is a healthy way to desire more, there is an unhealthy way. That unhealthy version is called *discontentment*, and it can be a sin. Discontentment can be tricky: not only is it one of those overlooked sins but it's also a fine line that's easily crossed.

Discontentment is more than groaning and complaining, though those are perfect indicators. "There are three sins that lie behind discontent—pride, rebellion, and unbelief. These are the original sins of the devil and his angels."[6] Here are some examples of what unhealthy discontentment can look like in us:

1. *Ugh, I can't believe God did that for her. He never gives me what I deserve.* This stems from a heart

that believes we know what's best for ourselves. (Hello, pride.)

2. Instead of accepting the sovereignty of God, you think, *He shouldn't have taken that away from me.* Or maybe you've wondered, *Why has God created me this way?* In other words, our hearts point to how God could've done a better job. Ouch. (Hello, rebellion.)

3. *God, are You up there? Are You actually doing anything? Do You not see my suffering? If You're not going to handle this, I will.* (Hello, doubt.)

Any of these statements resonate with you? At one point or another, we have all dealt with a bout of pride, rebellion, or doubt. Due to sin, it is our nature, but because of the cross, we can overcome. It's important we be in touch with our feelings and thoughts to figure out if there is a measure of discontentedness we feel, and then we must take it to God. He can work on that kind of ugly, too!

While the Lord works on the beautification process, it is Satan who perverts. He can take a raw and honest feeling you may have taken to God and twist it into an accusation you make *against* God. For example, I know God has called me to big things, but at the bottom (I understand it may not look like the bottom in your perspective), it's so hard to see. It just hurts. It's okay to feel that, but the enemy can take the hurt we feel and turn it into resentment. Perversion is our enemy's specialty. Stick with me, and I'll share how we can pinpoint his strategies and shift from discontentment to contentment in part 2.

Growing in Holiness

Don't you love when you come across a song that speaks directly to your spirit and situation? I have music playlists for different seasons of my life, and I can recognize what song meant what, when, and why. I remember the first time I heard "More" by Lawrence Flowers and was so moved I came up with choreography and ministered through dance at a few churches. I remember flowing so freely and with all that was within me. The lyrics spoke of freeing the worshiper in us from thoughts and anything else weighing us down. It spoke of giving more of ourselves to God because He's deserving of it all.

Then, there was "Satisfied" by The Walls Group. I remember hearing the lyrics, and I think it was the first time I'd felt so seen on a spiritual level. It was the first time I heard of a wanting for God in such a relatable way. A few years later, I sang the solo in my campus gospel choir, and it was a marked moment for me. That song spoke about how if I never get the things I desire on earth, ultimately, I just want to be satisfied with the Lord. And then there's a reversal! The artists go from asking themselves *if they will be satisfied* to telling the Lord they want to be satisfied with Him and then asking Him *if He will be satisfied* with them when getting to heaven. These songs comforted me when I found myself dwelling on the fears I mentioned in chapters 1 and 2.

Things looked extremely bleak and so eerily end times–ish at the start of the pandemic that I was reminded of a question I once asked myself. *Will I solely desire heaven simply because life on earth got too bad?* No, I want

Jesus for who He is. Truly, I desire to live out my days on earth looking forward to eternity in good times and bad.

I tried searching for an answer, an antidote for my mind. I would like to think I am fully submitted and surrendered to the sovereignty of God. I don't want to know all things; I accept that I won't always have the answers. I believe there is great peace in knowing that God makes all things beautiful in His time. I believe it makes the rough parts a little easier to bear. I also believe God gives us resources to help make sense of our situations. Those songs are prime examples and were the nudging of God in my early adulthood years. But I felt the Lord give me a full push when He led me to read *Growing in Holiness* by R. C. Sproul.

At the time, my mind had been telling me again, *Tarah-Lynn, clearly, something is wrong with you and you need Jesus. Go on and read this book. Grow in holiness, ya heathen!* So I read it and I did grow . . . out of that condemnation and into a realization that freed me. On the last day of a three-day fast I chose to do on a whim, I was reading the book and was blown away by the uniquely divine knowledge of God's Word that Sproul had.

Here's the journal entry I wrote on June 3, 2020:

Father, I've felt something was wrong with me for years because I wasn't "in love" with You. I would look at the faith of others (ya know, the ones that are so loud about it), and I began to think about how You might be withholding Your blessings from me because I don't love You as I should. But then You just spoke to me through this book. R. C. Sproul said, "Don't ask yourself, 'Do I love Christ perfectly?' Ask yourself, 'Do I love Him at all?'"[7]

It is enough that I have the desire and the request to experience You more intimately, love you more and love you better! Wow. Here I am thinking that the desire was wrong, that it should already exist with how far I am in my relationship with You.

The next line of the book asks, "Do I desire the triumph of Christ?"[8] My answer was yes, so I was good on that part, too. But then Sproul asked, "Do I look forward with joy to His coming?"[9] And to be honest, that answer is no and I don't know how to fix that. But I thank You, Lord, for showing me Your word in a new way.

In this chapter about justification (immediate upon belief) and sanctification (a life-long journey), You revealed how Satan is not only the tempter but the accuser and how You secured my salvation because my righteousness is in You alone. In reading that chapter, You taught me that I can't have the desire for righteousness or the desire to love You more unless love is already in my heart . . . unless I was already made alive by God the Holy Spirit (Rom. 5:5).

Love already lives in me! Thank you for your sweet confirmation. Satan tries to convince me that I'm "meh" and complacent but I'm seeing that Your love and Holy Spirit is within me day after day.

Talk about freedom! I felt a weight lift after reading that chapter. The healing process has already begun, and I believe that through *this* book, the Holy Spirit will activate something new in you. I've shared with you the fears and the feelings I was struggling with during the pandemic: *I will not be satisfied/experience joy in its fullness. There's*

something wrong with me. God does not fight for me.
I knew the truth, but my circumstances said otherwise.
Now, I will take you through an experience that changed
and renewed me forever.

Reflection Questions

1. In this chapter, I shared that when the COVID-19
   pandemic hit, I found it very difficult to be creative,
   which led to a loss of identity for me. Have you had
   a transitional time—either because of COVID or
   for some other reason—that led to a loss of identity for you? If so, how would you describe that?

2. Have you ever felt the need to "mute" some people
   on social media? If you did, what prompted that
   for you? Have you considered leaving social media
   completely?

3. "[God] is not disgusted or repulsed when He finds
   ungodliness within us; the Lord alone can do a
   beautification in us." Do you believe that? How
   does it make a difference for you to know that God
   is *partnering with you* in rooting out ungodliness
   rather than shaming you?

4. Are there songs, books, podcasts, etc. that you
   sense the Lord has pushed you toward because they
   will help you grow closer to Him in some way?
   Make a list of any that you know have helped you.

5. "Gratitude is a state of mind we must hold on
   to, and we must cling to it like it's all we've got."

Do you practice being grateful for something every day, or do you wait until something wonderful happens? If you focus on being grateful each day, how has that practice impacted your mental health?

4

The Purest Way

Defeating Evil Suggestions

Blessed are the pure in heart,
for they will see God.

Matthew 5:8 NIV

A constant prayer on my lips has been, *Lord, make me love You more than the world I know and see. Help me to love You more so You become all I see.* During the pandemic, I was a part of a Bible study group that did a deep study of spiritual gifts. The study opened me to a new view of how God works in believers—how He gives the *best* gifts and that we can effectively use them for His kingdom.

When I opened up about a spiritual gift I recently received, one of the members shared that my experience happened "in the purest way." That statement stood out to me because just the week prior, a close friend randomly praised me for having "such a pure heart." I've heard it from strangers, distant friends, and my mom (ha), but hearing it from my new friend at Bible study felt weighty. It got me thinking. And it was perfect timing, too, because I was given the assignment to lead the next Bible study session. I hadn't a clue what to teach on, but "pure" kept playing in my mind. I decided my study would be based on the Beatitudes, specifically focusing on Matthew 5:8, which says, "Blessed are the pure in heart, for they will see God."[1]

As I reflected on the verse, it hit me: the enemy has been bent on making me feel as if I won't see God. And not only that, I *shouldn't* see God.

He tried to convince me that the reason I'm not over the moon about heaven is because I'm horrible and belong in hell. He suggested that I have not seen the fulfillment of God's promises to me because there is something wrong with my heart. His goal was always to make me feel as if I was wicked. He would tell me I should back away from ministry because a negative emotion sprouted up. He would distort my Christ-given confidence and show me ways to dim it down because of those who see it as conceit. He would hint at how my boldness and bluntness belonged in certain parameters.

Baffled, I reflected on my childhood. I thought about the times I was considered "too cold" because I didn't cry or show weakness around others. I thought about how I was "too hard" because I had a temper and could happily go hours without speaking to someone I was upset with. I thought about how I was "too tough" if I was upset, hurt, or angry, and I didn't know how to express it except by keeping to myself. I thought about how I wasn't "soft enough" because I didn't know how to say sorry and, at times, felt as if I was right so I didn't have to.

But I was *a child* in age and in faith, and those accusations were all lies. And now here I am, a woman—flaws and all but standing in truth—being referred to as pure. That promise of Matthew 5:8 was and *is* for me! And queen, surely, it is for you.

The Heart Knows

What if I told you purity culture isn't just about sex? Please don't misunderstand: practicing abstinence before marriage matters, but purity is more than that. What if I told you that not only society gets it wrong but a lot of the time, the church gets it wrong, too?

As I was preparing for the Bible study I was to lead, there were so many precious moments when God kept ministering to me with assurance. "Yes, My sweet girl. You are so pure. Yes, I'm talking to you." I wanted to know exactly what He meant (and what my friends meant, too) so I did a deep dive on what purity truly is. The best place to begin is with the heart.

We often view the heart as a beautiful place that leads us into following our dreams, a place full of passions, affections, and truth. We refer to our heart as "the home of our emotions."[2] However, that is not how the Bible depicts it. As one writer explains, the Bible does not "distinguish between the head and the heart, combining the elements of mind, will, and emotions together with the language of an organ that can feel, think, and act."[3]

One of my favorite verses, Matthew 12:34, tells us that "the mouth speaks what the heart is full of."[4] In other words, what we speak gives us a glimpse of what is in our heart. It's a powerful vessel in numerous ways. Not only is our heart the power source of our lives physically but what we hold within it eventually makes its way out of us and has the power to speak life or death over us spiritually.

I like how Tim Keller describes it: "The heart is not just the seat of the emotions but also the source of our fundamental commitments, hopes, and trust. And from the heart flow our thinking, feelings, and actions. What the heart trusts, the mind justifies, the emotions desire, and the will carries out."[5]

The heart is a place that can be invaded with evil thoughts, murder, adultery, all sexual immorality, theft, lying, and slander. According to Matthew 15:18–19, these are all things that defile us. Society tells us to follow our heart, but we can't trust it.

In Jeremiah 17:9, the condition of our hearts is described as "the most deceitful of all things and desperately wicked." Jeremiah even questions, "Who really knows how bad it is?" In the New King James Version, Solomon dwells on a parallel idea: "Truly the hearts of the sons of men are full of evil; madness *is* in their hearts while they live."[6] This belief is consistent in the New Testament, as well. Romans 8:7 says, "For the sinful nature is always hostile to God. It never did obey God's laws, and it never will."

I know . . . yikes, right? It all may sound discouraging, but there's hope. The condition of our heart matters to God because He didn't just send His one and only Son on earth to die for bad habits or to see how well we can follow rules. Christ came for total transformation from the inside out; it's a purifying that only He can do.

The Lord peers into our heart and can truly see what it contains on full display. First Samuel 16:7 says, "Man looks at the outward appearance, but the LORD looks at the heart."[7] No one may know your deepest, darkest secrets, thoughts, and feelings, but God sees you for who you really are. He cares that we don't remain the same.

Faith versus the Hypocritical Heart

Jesus isn't a fan of hypocrites. We cannot be overly concerned with how we look on the outside when our insides tell a completely different story. We cannot have an air of self-importance when we all sin. We cannot puff up ourselves with religious rules and neglect our relationship with our Father.

In Matthew 23:25–26, Jesus says, "What sorrow awaits you teachers of religious law and you Pharisees. Hypocrites! For you are so careful to clean the outside of the cup and the dish, but inside you are filthy—full of greed and self-indulgence! You blind Pharisee! First, wash the inside of the cup and the dish, and then the outside will become clean, too."

Jesus is calling us to take the log out of our own eyes and pursue Him fully. Reforming the manners of society isn't the goal of Christ. Jesus is concerned with changing the manners of all hearts—the hypocritical ones, the not-so-hypocritical ones, everyone.

In the book of James, we learn that double-mindedness means choosing friendship with the world and, in turn, becoming enemies of God.[8] But to have a pure heart is to have an undivided heart; it is total allegiance to King Jesus. Jesus says, "Love the Lord your God with all your heart and with all your soul and with all your mind."[9]

The pure heart is not one in pursuit of selfish gain. Remember when I mentioned Jesus isn't a fan of hypocrites? In 1 Timothy 1:5, we see that believers are to be "filled with love that comes from a pure heart, a clear conscience, and genuine faith." I love how John Piper says, "God is the one who purifies the heart, and the instrument with which he cleans it is faith."[10]

God has called us to live just lives. First Peter 1:15–16 says, "But now you must be holy in everything you do, just as God who chose you is holy. For the Scriptures say, 'You must be holy because I am holy.'" None of us are perfect, but through Christ, we have the power to overcome what is evil and nothing like our God. Day by day, we can become more like Him. This life can be a difficult journey, but thank God, we have sanctification as our purification process. The cleaning agent of sanctification is activated through our obedience. The more we obey God's Word, the more we become like Christ—holy and faultless in every way.

I believe King David, known as the man after God's own heart, demonstrates what it best means to be pure. He shows us that purity is to truthfully seek the face of the Lord.[11] Even with all his mistakes, he pursued God. He sought God when he was scared, sought God when he was angry and rejected, sought God in repentance. I love how desperately honest he was; the book of Psalms ministers to me on so many levels! He knew what it meant to dwell in God's presence in good times and bad.

Again, purity does not equate to what the world deems perfection. Rather, it means we armor up against any sinful habits, thoughts, and actions and put them to death in order to come alive in Christ. His grace makes purity attainable. If it wasn't, Jesus wouldn't have mentioned it at all! If purity wasn't possible, we wouldn't be presented the opportunity to see God, as Matthew 5:8 promises.

To my lovely perfectionists out there, free yourself from that pressure! It is God *alone* who purifies us. He gives us grace for the times we fall and allows us into His presence to try again and again with Him. A pure heart is the willingness to change, the willingness to serve and obey. It is the willingness to ask God to search our heart, cleanse it, and lead us in everlasting ways.

Reflection Questions

1. What were you taught purity was supposed to look like?
2. What do you think Scripture means when it says the pure will "see God"?
3. How do you feel about the fact that God can see intimately inside your heart? Does that comfort you, frighten you, or bring up yet another emotion?
4. How can you invite the Holy Spirit to help you embrace His purification process?

5

A Walk with God

Trusting God Enough to Lead Your Way

For this reason I kneel before the Father, from whom every family in heaven and on earth derives its name. I pray that out of his glorious riches he may strengthen you with power through his Spirit in your inner being, so that Christ may dwell in your hearts through faith. And I pray that you, being rooted and established in love, may have power, together with all the Lord's holy people, to grasp how wide and long and high and deep is the love of Christ, and to know this love that surpasses knowledge—that you may be filled to the measure of all the fullness of God.

Ephesians 3:14–19 NIV

Do you journal? I used to take pride in how composed I could always be; I reveled in how I could use my fingers to count the few times I've cried. As you might expect, if it weren't for my journaling sessions throughout the last five years, I would have *definitely* found it difficult to express my thoughts and feelings. I've gone from expressing them all on paper to expressing them out loud . . . with wisdom, of course! If it weren't for journaling, I also wouldn't have this book! I hope my entries inspire you to be vulnerable with God and to expect Him to meet you in your quiet time.

Journaling at night is my favorite moment of peace. I call it my "Journal & Jesus" time, and it can last between thirty minutes and three hours. I tell my family that I'm unavailable, and when I retreat to my room, I hit "Do not disturb" on my phone, turn on soaking music, dim my lights, and from time to time, light my favorite candle. Then, I write. I sit and I reflect, I lie down, and I wait. I walk with God, line after line. I flow and I pause . . . over and over again until I feel everything that was in me is now out. Whether I'm sharing good news or I'm heavyhearted, if I don't "catch up" with God via journaling every few days, I feel incomplete and extremely unbalanced.

At 12:45 a.m. on the first of July in 2020, I experienced this imbalance again. I had spent too much time away from journaling and had recently returned to social media. Undoubtedly, I had a lot pent up. I penned,

Father, I don't know what the future holds but all I know is that I want to fully experience Your love and Your best for me. The other day, I realized that one of the reasons why Satan has been able to trip me up with comparisons lately is because I fear I won't be satisfied with Your best for me. But You know all I want is to find total satisfaction in You. I don't want to be so caught up in what You're doing in others that I can't celebrate who You are.

I really felt like I was losing it—day and night, the highlight reels of those who persecuted me were on replay and the previews of the blessings of my loved ones haunted me. I don't want to feel like I got the short end of the stick in life. I find myself daydreaming and I'm dissatisfied in the future and I hate that. Please remind me that the futures I dream up cannot compare. Save me from vain ambitions and reassure me that I am Yours.

I truly desire to feel loved, treasured, and the apple of Your eyes. I want to need and love you because there's no time left and there's no one I'd rather spend my days loving than You. I need You to saturate my mind and dissipate the lies and emptiness.

The ongoing struggle of visualizing an unsatisfactory future became overbearing when I found myself thinking about all the ways it could be possible. I didn't sense a response when I wrote the above, but it felt good to let those feelings out. I knew it was needed and sensed God was pleased with that moment of surrender. Every time I open my journal, I make a choice to give God my "yes" again. Even as I cry and my heart hurts . . . I will always say yes.

Journaling brings relief, and it can also reveal a lot about yourself. It shows where your sights lie. It aids you in measuring growth, recording the revelation God gives, and reflecting on the good and the bad. I always leave that time rejuvenated and ready to take on whatever comes next. When my fingers hurt, or if I feel I still need more time with God, I turn to other ways to commune.

Travel Therapy

Traveling is therapeutic for me and has saved me from a lot of heartache, but when the world closed for pandemic lockdowns, I had to rely heavily on journaling and taking walks around my neighborhood. Going outside and looking up at the vast sky always takes me back to gratitude. Communing with God that way reminds me just how big He is, how small I am, and how immeasurable His love is for me.

Depending on my mood, sometimes I choose a playlist and walk (and sometimes dance) to the beat of the music. Most times, I take in my surroundings and I allow nature to be my soundtrack. I walk in silence—with my ears open to the birds chirping, the splash of water in the nearby creek, the wisping away of leaves, and the whispers the Lord imprints upon my heart. The day after I wrote the entry above, I went for a walk. God didn't say anything then, just as with my journaling time. We just walked. Hand in hand, He led me.

While on that walk, I thought about my future and how I didn't quite know what God was calling me to do anymore. Don't get me wrong, I knew I was called, and I was aware of my giftings and could easily visualize the spheres of influence I could operate in. However, I realized that for the first time in my life, I wasn't certain in what capacity God would have me do things. I didn't know what or when that next step would happen.

I became more aware that I was just following God's lead. In previous seasons, I received hints and dreams and gentle nudging. I am naturally ambitious, and God

allowed me to just move. In the end, He showed me that
He was guiding me through my passions all along. But that
season was the first time I said, "I don't know." I didn't
know what was next for me. I concluded that there are
different means by which God leads depending on where
He situates us.

Not knowing can be adventurous or it can be pretty
scary, right? At that moment, it was both for me. I like
surprises from God, but not knowing anything at *all* made
me feel like I was out in the wild, susceptible to attack.
It made me feel like I was outside, eyes open but with no
clue where to go . . . But that's what faith is. Taking the
first step even when you don't grasp where you're going
but knowing that if you slip, God covers your fall. An un-
known future is scarier when we're not holding His hand.

When I returned home that evening, I took a shower
and reflected on the previous night's thoughts: my fear
of not agreeing with what God thinks is best for me. You
know how they say the shower is one of the best places
where inspiration strikes? Maybe there's something about
washing away our physical debris that causes God to find
the shower an opportune place to purify us from our spiritual debris, too.

In the shower, I remembered the words the Lord gave
me after a Bible study session on spiritual gifts: the "best
of the best." God made me realize that yes, I will give Him
my best. But most importantly, I can also count on Him
to do the same. God was telling me He wants to give *me*
the best of the best. He was assuring me that He *will* give
me the best of the best. I then prayed, "Lord, show me
how I can best trust You."

In that moment, He was saying, *Trust Me.* **It's true that sometimes we don't recognize the lies of the enemy because we don't know the truth of what God says, but I believe that we miss out on so much because we don't trust God as much as we should.** We trust Him in many ways, but He desires our trust in all ways, always.

Yes, Again. Trusting, Again.

In *Claim Your Crown*, I shared a funny little way God demonstrated to me that He would like for me to believe Him. I'm not going to spoil the story by giving you details but just know it involves an iridescent bracelet that had the word *believe* engraved on it. I received it as a gift, and there was a code that accompanied it, so I could swap bracelets with someone around the world once mine had served its purpose. It's truly a moment I won't ever forget! (You can learn that story in chapter 3, entitled "Heiress.")

Later, in a chapter I called "Queen of Hearts," I also wrote about the importance of service and how queens are not exempt from it. To illustrate this, I spoke about my last mission trip in Cuba. I shared how I fought to keep my "yes" to God when my responsibilities at home tempted me to say no.

On that trip, I not only had the opportunity to meet and serve God's amazing people, I also learned the history and influence of Haitians in Cuba. We traveled long hours to get to Camagüay, Guantánamo, Santiago de Cuba, Holguín, Las Tunas, and Havana in just ten days! Due to Cuba being a Communist country, we couldn't evangelize in the streets. "We had to rely on the Holy Spirit to guide us every step of the way in a foreign land. Not knowing what we'd be doing until we were led taught me to wait, to pray, to listen and then watch."[1]

What I *didn't* share in that book is that while I was at one of the last church services I attended on that trip, there was a young girl who took an interest in me . . . or shall I say, in my wrist. She looked to be eight years old or so. I was standing, singing along with my hands planted on the pew in front of me and would look down, smiling at her from time to time. Warmth filling her big brown eyes, she began to smile back and toy with my "believe" bracelet.

I knew what was happening. Do you know what was happening? Quick, before I go any further, take a guess. Okay, time's up—next thing you know, there was a nudging. God wanted me to give my bracelet to her!

I shared this story for the first time during a speaking engagement after I returned from the trip and explained to the audience how I wasn't being stingy, but still, as I pondered on whether or not God was leading me to give it to her, my mind was like, *Lord, but this is mine; You gave me this reminder and it's been helping me even here!*

And then I tricked the audience into believing that I didn't give it to the little girl. The audible gasp was *hilarious*, and it was even funnier when they realized I was kidding. (I'm totally smiling as I write this, by the way. Okay, now I'm snickering as I think about what my family's reactions will be when they hear of this story and the joke for the first time. Such a great trick!)

On a serious note, don't we do that with the stuff God gives us? We say, "This is mine" almost as if He won't provide more or He won't give better . . . as if He won't give the best. It's a poverty mindset. God's trying to loosen those clenched fists of ours. He desires open hands and an open heart. What are you bringing to God today? What have you been holding on to?

As I write this, I'm reminded what I shared that day at the speaking engagement. When I gave the little girl the bracelet, I remembered, *It's not about you.* And to begin to come out of that mindset, we need to let go of not only the sin that so easily entangles but also the things that aren't sin but that we're still so wrapped up in. Things like . . . our idea of what our futures should look like, or maybe, I don't know . . . struggling with *believing* we'll be satisfied with the promises God has reserved for us.

I knew I had to give my bracelet to her. I didn't need to switch with someone else; the bracelet had served its purpose. Besides, no way was I going to deny a little girl a gift, and there was absolutely no way I was going to deny God! Can you imagine the regret I would feel flying back to the States? No, thanks. After the service, I placed the bracelet on the little girl's wrist, and she grinned so wide. She ran off with her friends to show off her new "believe" bracelet, and they watched as the stones glinted and turned colors underneath the hot sun.

The Blessing

The day before our departure, my church's missionary group gathered one last time to reflect and pray with Pastor Jacinto, our vivacious, eighty-something, Holy Spirit–filled guide whom I affectionately call my grandpa and still am in contact with. We were hugging goodbyes to the pastors and guides after our final prayer meeting, and as some were beginning to disperse, Pastor Jacinto halted. Everyone stopped what they were doing and watched. Almost instinctively, he laid his hands on my head and blessed me. He spoke words over my life that I needed to hear, and the room was in shock. He admitted later the Lord would not let him leave until he blessed me.

More than two years later, I'm still a bit speechless, but what I can say is, I traveled home fully aware of God's favor, love, and attention. I was encouraged and reminded of not just God's plans for my life but how He was so mindful of my current needs. I realized that there was so much pushback against me going on this trip because the enemy wanted to keep me from being a blessing and receiving that blessing.

When I returned home, my literary agent told me that I landed a triple book deal! A few weeks later, I won second runner-up in a national pageant and was crowned the Heart Truth Champion for raising awareness of heart health. (I chuckle at that title and consider how God knew we'd be talking about the spiritual state of the heart here. He's so funny.) I had no PR representative, no pageant training, no state director. It was all God. I'm not saying my obedience got me the book deal or my standing in the pageant. God's grace did. But I'm saying obedience and trusting God when we can't see will light the path before us.

Something else is coming, something bigger. The number eight shows me that. (By the way, peeps, numerology, angel numbers, and all that stuff is ungodly—that's not at all what I'm referring to here.) It wasn't until recently that

I discovered the number eight biblically symbolizes new beginnings. Today, I don't hold it closely, so I don't allow the enemy an entry to easily distort and derail God's plan for my life by confusing me with his "signs." However, back then, God dropped the number eight in my life in such creative ways.

I launched the *Dressed for Battle* podcast on 8/8/18, not knowing why but knowing the date was special. When the pageant contestant order was released, I discovered I was number 18. While at the pageant, I received an $8 donation with the message "new beginnings." And the final night, as I reached into the bowl for my numbered question, I opened the piece of paper and saw the number 8 scribbled on it. My spirit leaped. My mouth was agape. All I could say was, "I hear You, Jesus. Thank You."

As I walked across that stage one last time, the presenter read aloud one of the key passages that sustained me in that season: Isaiah 43:18–19. "Forget the former things; do not dwell on the past. See, I am doing a new thing! Now it springs up; do you not perceive it? I am making a way in the wilderness and streams in the wasteland."[2] I remembered, no matter the outcome, God utilized this platform to elevate me further. That pageant may not have been my "new thing," but it sure is here, in Jesus's name.

Our reward is coming. We have to believe that. Whether our sacrifice is big or small, we will be rewarded for it. Whether it is obvious or one that only we know about, we will be rewarded for it. God sees what we put on hold to tend to His instructions. He sees what we give up for His glory. He does not overlook our obedience; He will honor our sacrifice. We *need* to believe that. I know I do.

Reflection Questions

1. I almost didn't serve on the Cuba trip because of the competing demands on my time at home, but despite that pushback, my time there was a blessing to both me and others. Where are you seeing pushback in your own life right now? What kind of blessing might arise if you persist in the direction you feel called to go in spite of that pushback?

2. What does trusting God look like for you? Where do you struggle in your trust journey?

3. What discipline can you utilize to express to God that you desire His will over your way?

6

Birthdays and Battlefields

The Power of Self-Denial

You will keep him in perfect peace,
Whose mind is stayed on You,
Because he trusts in You.

Isaiah 26:3 NKJV

October 24 is a holiday in my house. Every day is a blessing, yes, but I wholeheartedly believe every human being should feel especially treasured on their special day. Hence, my birthday is a *big* deal for me.

I celebrate the whole month of October with the works: treating myself to my favorite restaurants, less work and more rest, intentional time with entertainment, shopping for my birthday outfit, deciding whether or not I'll travel (and if so where), planning my birthday photo shoot, choosing where I'll have my celebration dinner, and more.

Truly, it's a whole process, and I look forward to it every year.

What I don't look forward to are the anxiety, headaches, and stomach pains that come prior to the festivities. It didn't help that all these things were amplified since I had plenty of time to be alone with my thoughts when COVID hit.

In October 2020, a couple signs led me to a solution for dealing with the heaviness that always seems to find its way to me when I aim to celebrate. It was a solution I never considered: the Daniel Fast. In Daniel 1, we learn the biblical story of a strong, healthy, good-looking, and gifted son of nobility who was taken captive along with other young men and positioned for training under King Nebuchadnezzar's reign.

In preparation for the young men's eventual entry into the royal service, the king assigned them rich delicacies from his very own kitchen. We're talking the finest meats, wine, dairy—you name it. However, devoted to honoring his faith, Daniel proposed a test to the chief official. For ten days, Daniel and his three friends would consume vegetables and water and would be compared to the other young men who were on the king's diet. They came out way stronger and more nourished than their counterparts; their results inspired the same diet for all the other young men in training.

When I first told my mother I would be doing the Daniel Fast, she asked me, "Daniel who?!" We both laughed so hard, especially because she was definitely 75 percent serious. I complimented her, exclaiming, "That was a good one!" I'd heard of the Daniel Fast numerous times before, but I never felt led to do it or do more research about it.

You see, I eat meat with *every* meal; I feel incomplete without it. I'm not a fish person, and unlike my siblings, seafood is not my first choice. Plus, I live in a Haitian household with amazing cuisine. My mother's a great cook and my dad's a chef—can you blame me?!

Today, the Daniel Fast lasts between ten and twenty-one days and includes fruits, vegetables, whole grains, beans, and water. Seeing this, I was surprised I didn't balk at the venture ahead, but it was chapter 10 of the book of Daniel that further piqued my interest.

Fasting was a lifestyle for Daniel. He sincerely pursued God for repentance; he stood in the gap for his people and received revelation through the visions God gave him. In Daniel 10, we find the Old Testament prophet practicing self-denial again as he sought an answer from God through fasting and prayer for twenty-one days. David Guzik writes,

> The correlation between Daniel's time of self-denial and prayer and the duration of the battle between the angels and the prince of the kingdom of Persia establishes a link between Daniel's prayer and the angelic victory. Since the angelic victory came on the 21st day, we can surmise that if Daniel would have stopped praying on the 20th day, the answer may not have come.[1]

Powerful, huh? Other confirmations aligned to reinforce that I had to commit myself to this fast. I knew I needed to practice this form of self-denial. I *knew* I needed rescue.

Let's take a minute: How ironic is it that God had me dedicate myself to sacrifice in a month I usually dedicate to myself? I felt it in my bones: this fast would be totally different than the intermittent ones I'd done before. I felt God calling me to come out of where I was and to enter His presence in a new way. I needed change, so I began my journey. I wanted God to show me what I was truly longing for.

Spiritual Boot Camp

I have many quirks—some of them wisely developed over time in order to guard my heart. Here's one: I love to celebrate people at my core, but I don't watch testimonies on YouTube unless I feel led. God is so great, and He does miraculous works. I 100 percent believe He will do it for you. But I'm careful watching testimony videos because I am familiar with God's technique for me.

Oftentimes when God leads me to do something, I don't get the optimal result I desire . . . yes, even in the waiting. It often feels as if I have the breakthrough the hard way. There's always an extra step with me. So as I embarked on this fast, half of me was like, "He won't do something crazy miraculous for me because He *always* makes me take the long road."

Don't get me wrong: God has done mind-blowing instantaneous things in my life. However, they were things I didn't ask for or could never dream up—they were all surprises that I'm ridiculously grateful for (like the opportunity to speak to you through my books)! But in regard to the things I *do* ask for? Man . . . it can make me question if He cares about what's on my heart at all.

My journal entry on October 3, 2020, reads:

For stuff I didn't ask for, You go all out with surprising me but for struggles that have lasted years, You take your time. While I would appreciate a speedy breakthrough after persevering just this once, I am really just here to spend time with You, Lord . . . I'm expecting greater intimacy. It would be great to have been given newfound joy in You but as I thought of that and wrote it out . . . I realized I didn't fully believe that could happen in a 21 day fast when I've been wanting this for years.

When you recognize how God deals with you, you're prone to remembering how your journey is unlike anyone else's (and not necessarily in a bad way). And when I'm committing to anything that will lead me into greater intimacy with Him, I don't ever want to compare and say, "You did it for this person when they fasted . . . How come You didn't do it for me?" I understand fasting is powerful; however, I also understand God deals differently with each of His children.

Therefore, I didn't binge on an all-you-can-eat buffet of Daniel Fast testimony videos, nor did I fast particularly for one thing or several things. I made a list of my concerns and pain points and brought them to God in expectancy, but I did not have tunnel vision on my requests. I told myself that even if God didn't do anything for me, I was sure this would be a training in some way. Phew, and what a training it was!

It was my very first Daniel Fast, and there I was, reaching for the stars and committing to twenty-one days. Spoiler alert: I didn't last! I quickly realized that ten days sounded just about right. But we'll get to that part of the story later.

The Necessities of Life

The first thing I did was minimize my surroundings. Though I did the Daniel Fast for ten days, I fasted from social media for twenty-one days. Throughout it all, I committed to a Proverbs 31 Ministries study that was released right in time for my fast. And get this: it was called *The Answers to Your Deepest Longings.*

I listened to soaking music and prophetic podcasts, studied the book of Daniel, read books, journaled my journey every day and every night. I would lie awake, speaking to God. I told Him how I was feeling, and I asked Him what He would like to do with where I was. Because of the pandemic, I wasn't traveling anymore, and at the time, I didn't have any pressing deadlines for my devotional or any digital fashion campaigns. I had space in my schedule for "me time" . . . the superconscious, self-denied version, I should say.

I remember on day one of the fast, I busted out laughing after looking for a taste of sweetness in my morning oatmeal (it was nowhere to be found, by the way). The first few days, my stomach would cramp up from time to time, and I'd go to bed early after I went through all of my activities and found I was just plain bored. On occasion, God awakened me from my sleep with ideas of what to eat: plantains, sweet potatoes, and avocados—I forgot I loved those!

Throughout this process, my mother helped by preparing most of my meals. I was trying my best, but yeah, she knew I was suffering! It helped that not only was she helping me focus on the fast and not the food but she was always cheering me on day after day.

On day four, I exclaimed, "Lord, I can't do this without You." I was miserable, y'all. Absolutely gutted. Gutted and hungry. With every veggie-spooned bite, I fought thoughts of meat and every dramatic claim of "I'm not going to make it." I had to ask God to show me why I was doing this. I spoke aloud but I also wrote:

> Lord, I wonder if I'm doing this fast right. Shouldn't I feel closer to You? I desire a radical shift. I desire an encounter that'll change me forever. I'm fighting the idea that I'm missing out because it's my month (that You gave teehee) and I'm not going all out for me. It's the only time I treat myself so freely and whenever I look at the calendar, I just see so many days ahead with nothing to look forward to. I don't know how You will show up for me—if You will in the way I want. Yes, I know You will in the ways that I **need** but it would be nice to not have to go through excruciating toil, wait, and pain for a felt need to be addressed.

On day eight, I realized, this is how God wants me to feel about life . . . being extremely cognizant of my need for Him in every passing moment, I mean. I would lose my mind if I focused on my dreams and aspirations instead of focusing on who God is and what He wants to do through me.

Have you reflected on your need for God lately? I feel as though we as Christ-followers behave as if the God-shaped hole within us was completely filled when we invited Him into our lives. Or that the void we were created with can be filled *only* when we meet our Maker. But we often forget that we can meet Him here on earth as it is in heaven every day.

The desperate need we recognized when we experienced salvation can morph into a brand-new form of desperation for Christ as we live out our lives in this world.

Reflection Questions

1. Are you able to identify a specific pattern for how God "deals with you"? If so, how would you describe that?

2. When was the last time you genuinely expressed to God, *I can't go a moment without You*?

3. Have you done any type of fast before? There are so many types of fasts (water only, the Daniel Fast, no sugar, etc.). How did God sustain you?

4. My mom's help preparing meals and cheering me on made a huge difference in my Daniel Fast. Can you think of a way another believer has helped you persevere in reaching a spiritual goal? If so, what was your goal, and how did they help you?

7

The Shift

*Embracing the Not-So-Secret Weapon
That Changes Everything*

Create in me a clean heart, O God,
And renew a steadfast spirit within me.
Psalm 51:10 NKJV

Point out anything in me that offends you,
and lead me along the path of everlasting life.
Psalm 139:2

"Your day is coming, Tarah-Lynn," my mother declared.
"Your day is coming." The next morning, I heard her praying outside of my bedroom, asking God to have mercy on me and to take notice of me. I hadn't yet awakened fully but I heard her prayer, encouraging me to keep serving the Lord because "He will come through." He did.

To better equip my mind as I prepared for the Daniel Fast, I picked a book from my personal library to read. I chose a book I'd had for years but for some reason, never opened. It was *Battlefield of the Mind* by Joyce Meyer.[1]

It took me a little while to get into it, but I had a knowing that I had to keep going. Soon enough, I sensed God was showing me why He had me do this fast. The enemy must've sensed I was close, too, because I had a strange nightmare the first day of the fast.

As I read the book, I realized I had accepted that I would just struggle with not being 100 percent excited about eternity. The book helped me discern it was wrong for me to think I would have to deal with that until I get to heaven when God could release me from it *now*. I could begin a part of the process *now*. Healing comes from Christ, but it begins with us.

Have you accepted wrong thoughts? As warriors of God's royal army, we have the power to defeat the enemy and conquer strongholds. The Passion Translation of 2 Corinthians 10:5 tells us that our Commander and King has given us the weapons to "demolish every deceptive fantasy that opposes God and break through every arrogant attitude that is raised up in defiance of the true knowledge of God. We capture, like prisoners of war, every thought and insist that it bow in obedience to the Anointed One." You hear that? We can demolish, we can break through, we can drag our thoughts to their knees.

You see, it wasn't just wrong that I accepted the thought that I will be dissatisfied (and in turn, accepted defeat) but it was actually *sinful* to think that "it would always be this way." What's so funny is that right before I opened *Battlefield of the Mind*, I googled "the right mindset for Daniel Fast" and followed a couple of links. Immediately,

God pointed out two things to me. The word *repent* in the Greek language is defined as to "change the way you think."[2] This was revelatory for me. God immediately confirmed that changing my mind was what He wanted to do, and it's not a cop-out result that I'm relying on just because there was a "chance" He wouldn't do everything else for me in this fast. To be honest, it was all I needed! Blown away, I wrote:

> I need to repent, Lord. I typically thought of repentance as turning away from old ways and sins, but it was revelation to me that it also included giving You all of my thoughts. In this quarantine, I had my mind flooded over my future . . . ideas of great things happening but me never feeling satisfaction. I am so sorry, Lord. I repent and I give you the roots of those feelings.

I felt so free . . . my mind was opened. And I also realized this: I didn't even know I was being wounded by the attacks in that season! Because I've been aware that spiritual warfare is real and there's indeed a battle over our minds (hello, Priscilla Shirer's *Fervent*), I didn't consider myself a victim. How could I experience injuries if I was informed of the battle and armored to fight? I knew the enemy inflicts fear, but the truth of those negative thoughts about dissatisfaction felt natural—like they were just my own ordinary thoughts.

Maybe you've thought the same? Maybe you thought, *Ugh, why am I thinking like this? My mind feels like it's going to explode.* Or, *It's not like I can just start over.* And to that I ask, or *can* you? I'm referring to the spiritual sense, people! The New International Version of

Romans 12:2 says, "Do not conform to the pattern of this world, but be transformed by the renewing of your mind."

Like me, you probably have heard or seen that verse over the course of your Christian life. It's fairly popular. I committed that verse to memory as a child, but as I was in my mess at that moment, I realized that "renewal" felt like a concept. Renewal became real for me only when I experienced revelation.

I like the New Living Translation of Romans 12:2. It instructs you to "let God transform you into a new person by changing the way you think." Even as I type this out, I'm blown away! When the Lord showed me how wrong I was about my thinking, I was like, "Whoa, so You mean I don't have to stay here?" And He was like, "Nope!" And I was like, "You want to change the way I think?!" And He was like, "Yup!" So, I say the same to you. You don't have to be a prisoner of your mind; I'll show you how to break off those shackles and run free.

The Truth Filter

Freedom starts with what I am calling "the shift." The shift is a realization that leads to repentance. I made a cool acronym so we can reference it from here on out: see harmful ideations fall (with the) truth (of God). The other version I created was she heals ideations (in the) face (of) truth. They both essentially mean and spell the same thing, but let's stick with the official one, shall we? I'm a visual person, so I thought it would be better to show you how it looks.

See
Harmful
Ideations
Fall (with the)
Truth (of God)

According to Merriam-Webster, an ideation is "the capacity for or the act of forming or entertaining ideas."[3] Ideations can be positive or negative. However, I believe neither will stand true if they are filtered through the Word of God.

You see, sis, the Lord doesn't leave us out here defenseless. His Word is a weapon! The Passion Translation of 2 Corinthians 10:3–4 lets us know that though "we live in the natural realm, we don't wage a military campaign employing human weapons, *using manipulation to achieve our aims*. Instead, our *spiritual* weapons are energized with divine power to effectively dismantle the defenses *behind which people hide*."

The Good News is not a reel that gets old as we live out our lives; it is necessary in every season to bring about conviction, grace, forgiveness, and power. Nothing can stand against the Word of God—not even the thoughts that seem ingrained in your mind. The Word of the Lord "will even penetrate to the very core of our being where soul and spirit, bone and marrow meet! It interprets and reveals the true thoughts and secret motives of our hearts."[4] The NIV says it "is alive and active" and "sharper than any double-edged sword"! How beautifully relieving it is to have a weapon that does not tarnish or dull. The Word of God is the best weapon in our arsenal, leading us to glory.

Let's draw our attention back to the shift. For the shift to occur, we must first see or identify the thought. Capture it. Distinguish it. If the ideation, imagination—whatever you want to call it—is indeed sinful, you will be a witness to how it doesn't stand a chance once it is filtered through the truth of God. Then, repentance will be born in that place.

The King of Our Hearts

I've mentioned repentance a couple times already, but now let's define it in a way that will speak most to our current situation. "Repentance is not just part of the transformation by which a sinner becomes a saint, but is an attitude of heart, with accompanying actions, that should mark the whole of a believer's life."[5]

Repentance is a crucial building block to living and *staying* free. Think about how we come to God initially. We first accept Christ into our lives because we recognize our need for Him, and we repent because we're immediately made aware of a wrong that can be made right only by our Savior. When we change the way we think about things, a brand-spanking-new life is made accessible to us. When we are born-again, the kingdom of God resides within us.[6] It is *found* in us. However, we often don't experience the peace that the King of our hearts brings because we merge the old with the new. The transformation is found in the renewal experience.

In Joel 2:12–13, the Lord says, "Turn to me now, while there is time. Give me your hearts. Come with fasting, weeping, and mourning. Don't tear your clothing in your grief, but tear your hearts instead." In those times, the Lord's people would often tear their clothes to display their grief and sorrow after they'd disobeyed or experienced great loss. (Take the Israelites or Job, for example.) That was their custom then, but it is not what the Lord expects of us now. Can you imagine tearing apart our clothes every time we sinned?! We'd have nothing to wear!

Yes, God no longer instructs us to tear our clothes. Rather, He tells us not to be so caught up in changing our appearance or our outward conduct. That won't bring about the change that matters. With unrepentance, the heart is the problem. When the heart is unchanged, any behavioral adaptations are only short-term. God desires for our hearts to be so moved that necessary internal change comes. This includes our thoughts, beliefs, attitudes, motives, desires . . . all of it! The process starts with repentance.

Change is the first step to something even greater. In the rest of verse 13, the Lord encourages us to return to Him "for he is merciful and compassionate, slow to get angry and filled with unfailing love. He is eager to relent and not punish." Let's run to the Father, because there is hope waiting for us once we open the door to a repentant life.

When we ask God to show us any form of rebellion, unconfessed sin, or unforgiveness, He will reveal it. And when we confess it, He forgives it. There is no reason to fear. The great thing about confessing sinful thoughts or any sin at all for that matter is the fact that we can go directly to the Father, and we can do so with confidence! We will receive mercy and discover grace in our time of need. Hebrews 4:14–16 says,

Now that we know what we have—Jesus, this great High Priest with ready access to God—let's not let it slip through our fingers. We don't have a priest who is out of touch with our reality. He's been through weakness and testing, experienced it all—all but the sin. So let's walk right up to him and get what he is so ready to give. Take the mercy, accept the help.[7]

Sis, I'm taking *all* the mercy and accepting *all* the help—how about you?!

Our Words Are Heard

Want to know something funny?

After I put aside the book and laid in bed that first night of the Daniel Fast, I flipped over and my attention was drawn to a small canvas art one of my siblings purchased at Target and hung on the wall of my grandmother's room. (My grandmother was away, visiting family in Haiti, during the time of my fast, so I left my bedroom and slept in hers.) I'd either awaken to the canvas or fall asleep with it being the last thing I read. That night as I read it, I laughed aloud.

Written on the canvas was Isaiah 26:3: "You will keep in perfect peace those whose mind is stayed on you." Isn't. That. *Nuts*? God had been working on my thinking since day one! He was all up in my face–or head–the whole time! I just love His humor; His jokes are knee-slappers.

I'm incredibly grateful for all the ways God showed Himself to me during that experience. My Daniel Fast testimony is unlike many because it doesn't speak to the outward manifestations of the fast but to what God has done inwardly. When God can do a work *in* you, He can do so much more outside of you. Submitting your insides provides Him room to use you. The Lord transformed my mind, and I was strengthened in my weakness.

God taught me a number of things during this fast, and you'll see more of what I learned sprinkled through the rest of this book. Before we go any further, I would like to share this last thing: I pride myself in being a disciplined individual, but I could not complete the full twenty-one days of this fast. I say this shamelessly! I had high hopes, but I needed more than hopes to make it through. I was able to stay in solitude, remain off social media, and all of that, but doing the Daniel Fast as a first-timer and on a *whim* was extremely difficult.

A few days into the fast, I asked God if I could do it for ten days instead, and His response brought me peace. In that moment, I learned that the Lord saw how desperately I long for Him, and He honored my sacrifice and willingness. It was enough. If you have a desire to do this fast but you're afraid of "failing," or if you've tried this fast before and you gave in just as soon as you started, do not beat yourself up. God isn't doing that!

I'm not encouraging you to say "God knows my heart" and quit or make excuses. I am saying be free of your past and mentally and spiritually prepare for your future. The Lord is waiting to meet you right where you are. Your experience of the Daniel Fast will look different than mine, and that is entirely okay! Allow God to speak to you the way He knows is best *for you*. One thing is for sure: when we deny ourselves physically, our spiritual senses are heightened. With regular praying and fasting, you'll find yourself crossing over into a new spiritual dimension where you are intimate with the Lord, sensitive to the Holy Spirit's direction, and open to change.

If it feels like you've been waiting for your breakthrough forever, I especially encourage you to do this fast and bring that pain point to God in prayer. From the very first day we speak, our words are heard in heaven. In Daniel's case, he wasn't informed of this until the last day, when help actually came. Today, we can pray with certainty that God hears us and dispatches heavenly assistance when we call on His name.

But sometimes, there *is* a delay. At times, God chooses to have us wait (so in actuality, it's no delay at all). Sometimes, we don't see our promises because *we* get in our own way. And then there are times when our promises are delayed due to demonic attack. Ask the Lord if there's anything He desires to reveal to you about yourself, any strongholds in your past, and/or what is happening in the spiritual realm, and believe that He will answer with what He desires to reveal. We can search our hearts ourselves, but only God can make known to us the evils that lie there. Pray Psalm 139:24: "Point out anything in me that offends you, and lead me along the path of everlasting life." He will do it.

No one likes to hear this (hello, self), but God allows difficulty for His purpose and our good. For example, in Daniel's situation, an angel informed him that he was carrying the answers Daniel sought "but for twenty-one days the spirit prince of the kingdom of Persia blocked my way."[8] The angel was fighting that entire time and even had to call for backup!

God could have blasted the demonic forces into oblivion, but He chose not to. Daniel didn't know there was a fight unleashed, preventing his victory; he just knew to persevere in prayer. Now, can you imagine "how much angelic assistance or insight has never been realized, or greatly delayed, because of a lack of persistence in prayer [in us]?"[9] There are times that help doesn't immediately come because the Lord is developing us into women of valor and prayer—women after His own heart.

I don't know about you, but all this talk about fighting is getting me riled up. Are you ready to snatch back the peace the enemy stole? Are you prepared to train your mind to rule your thoughts? Part 2 is built upon verse 6 of 2 Corinthians 10. The Passion Translation says, "*Since we are armed with such dynamic weaponry*, we stand ready to punish any trace of rebellion, as soon as you choose complete obedience." I will show you how to prevail over the enemy and punish sinful thoughts—not yourself. Armor up, queen. Let's get dressed for battle.

I hope my testimony birthed or fed a longing in your heart to draw near to God. If you're feeling distant from Him, I can promise you He longs to have you near Him. He longs to be with you. And He honors your desire to connect with Him. He can help you in your journey to kingdom thinking. I share my full Daniel Fast testimony on my YouTube channel, Adorned in Armor. Scan the QR code for the direct link!

Reflection Questions

1. Have you accepted any "wrong thoughts" about yourself or God? If so, are these simply inaccurate, or are they sinful?

2. Do you believe God can heal your mind by transforming it (Rom. 12:2)? If so, have you asked Him to do that?

3. I shared my SHIFT acronym with you. What ideations/imaginations might you need to expose to God's truth?

4. Have you asked God to reveal any weaknesses or strongholds in you? What do you need to repent of? How does Hebrews 4:14–16 give you courage to do that?

PART 2

COMBAT

8

Defying Our Minds and Personalities

Character is both developed and revealed by tests, and all of life is a test.

Rick Warren, *The Purpose Driven Life:*
What on Earth Am I Here For

People often tell me I am one of the most positive people they have ever met. I'd like to *think* so, too. (Ha, get it? This is the first time I used a pun, so laugh along, will ya?) I regularly describe myself as an optimist with a dash of realism. Because of this, I didn't second-guess my thought patterns.

When Joyce Meyer said, "Think about what you think about,"[1] she changed the game for us all. Satan doesn't want us to be conscious about the lies we meditate on! It's one thing to know we are in a spiritual war; we equip ourselves to fight. It's another to be unaware of the enemy's tactics zeroed in on your mind.

I wonder if what comes next will blow your mind just as much as it did mine when I read *Battlefield of the Mind*. Here goes: the "obvious" sinful thoughts (hateful, perverted, etc.) aren't the only ones that are dirty. Sinful thoughts include thoughts that are just straight up wrong. Sinful thoughts include thoughts that are not true. Not only that, negative thinking is not the sole category for negative thoughts![2]

Let me break this down. When we use negative as an adjective, we mean something is cynical or bleak . . . the very opposite of optimism and all things positive, right? However—and this just came to me now but maybe you mathematical and law geniuses were already thinking this—when we use negative as a noun, it denotes a contradiction. It's false. What I'm trying to say is just because the thought isn't negative, doesn't mean it is not wrong! **If my thoughts go against the nature of God, if they do not honor God, if they contradict the truth of God, then they keep me away from God.**

And get this: the enemy can even use rationalizing to confuse us. Satan can't read our minds, but he's been around us long enough to know us. He watches us closely, ya know? He knew that while I am a positive person, I am one who leans to logic; I am prone to embrace the facts. He would disguise himself in realistic scenarios that made my vision foggy. Facts became my truth, and I didn't know the difference. I knew he was causing the dissatisfaction, but I didn't see how he was infiltrating my thoughts. I thought those were just me.

I didn't know sinful thoughts included the very thing I was suffering from: the belief that I would just have to live like this, and I would be dissatisfied in the future. That means sinful thoughts include the belief that God won't do His best for me—no, that I won't consider His work as best.

The scales fell from my eyes with that one. Phew, I was so grateful for that revelation. It was so freeing to read and recognize that this is what I was doing! This was a problem. My concepts, or the scenarios that played out in my head, were realistic in nature, so it was easy for me to think these scenarios were harmless because of how much they made sense. And so, these thoughts would dampen my spirit even as I tried to figure out ways to protect myself from those situations or my own heart.

Remember how I mentioned that I was well aware and relieved that my spirit longed for heaven, but was confused as to why my mind sometimes didn't? 1 Corinthians 2:14 tells us that "people who aren't spiritual can't receive these truths from God's Spirit. It all sounds foolish to them and they can't understand it, for only those who are spiritual can understand what the Spirit means." I was so confused because I wasn't being fed God's truth, and I didn't even notice how my natural man was thriving off of my logic and reasoning. So of course, I would be attacked with anxious thoughts about eternity if Satan already had made himself a home in my thoughts and delighted in making that fear a playground.

When you know better, you do better, right? I just realized all I did was rationalize, or what I'll call "rational lies." It was too easy for those lies to make sense. I didn't notice it in the moment, but I know this now and can recognize it going forward. To dispel those lies and ultimately shift my thinking, I can ask how those ideations align with the truth of God. They won't! For example, my thought was, *There's a chance I won't be happy in the future.* And I made rational lies for how this could be true since I have many struggles in my life now. But I am a witness to how the lie has to bow to the truth of God. He's been good in my suffering now, and He will be good then.

In Matthew 7:11, the truth says, "If you, imperfect as you are, know how to lovingly take care of your children and give them what's best, how much more ready is your heavenly Father to give wonderful gifts to those who ask him?"[3] The truth proves I have a Father who gives the best gifts. Ephesians 3:20 reminds us, "Now all glory to God, who is able, through his mighty power at work within us, to accomplish infinitely more than we might ask or think." The truth proves that the God I serve can blow my mind with miracles I could never imagine. The New American Standard Bible version of James 1:17 declares, "Every good thing given and every perfect gift is from above, coming down from the Father of lights, with whom there is no variation or shifting shadow." The truth says my Father not only gives in perfection, He is perfection! He does not change; He remains the same . . . steadfast in love, steadfast in giving, steadfast in shining.

When I encounter the truth, I can repent from my false thoughts. I have the power to shift. When I shift, I am reminded it is sinful to meditate on thoughts that are wrong. When I shift, I am reminded that if my mind does stay on those thoughts, then I can spin them to thoughts that are positive. Better yet, I can spin them to thoughts that honor God.

After reading about Joyce Meyer's season of disbelief and how God revealed that the culprit was "mind-bending spirits,"[4] I rebuked them in the name of Jesus and invited the spirit of wisdom, peace, and revelation in their place. This is your moment to do the same, sis! Rebuke what has been tormenting you, and invite the Lord to saturate your mind with His goodness.

Seeing God

One of the activities I did during my Daniel Fast was listen to *Exploring the Prophetic* with Shawn Bolz. In his interview with Steffany Gretzinger, I found God and a couple of aha moments. Isn't it so funny when you think you're doing something because of personal interest and God meets you in it?

In that episode, I thought I was just going to learn about going deeper in worship, and instead I received a revelation about myself and fasting. Shawn asked Steffany, "What's the riskiest thing God ever had you do?" And she spoke about how God had to retrain her thoughts. It was so descriptive! Shawn responded, "Your language mentors people's thought processes."[5] Isn't that such a beautiful way to say, "You explain what people are thinking?!"

Shawn quoted Matthew 5:8 to exemplify the beauty of a mind being used by God. Remember when I shared how God gave me Matthew 5:8 earlier this summer? Well, in this episode, Shawn shared the Message version, which says, "You're blessed when you get your inside world—your mind and heart—put right. Then you can see God in the outside world."

It was confirmation that God was dealing with my thoughts, but it also reminded me of a word I received a couple months ago: I must re-educate the intellect. I literally was like "wowww" and had to pause the interview. They continued talking about their journeys and how they'd needed change in their emotional and spiritual thought lives. God met me in that conversation.

In a season when I felt I was constantly being let down, God told me this: "I am not trying to embarrass you." I would keep this in mind as I pursued my big dreams, but there were still small parts of me that felt like God was going to play me. In the interview, Shawn shared that as a practical person, he had to learn a very important lesson—it's one I needed to hear and felt like God was calling me out with! If we hold back from sharing the God-sized dream, then we won't be able to celebrate the miracle fully when it does happen. And if we hold back from sharing the God-sized dream and the miracle doesn't happen, we won't heal. We have to share our hopes and expectancy with courage, knowing that regardless of the outcome, the Lord is with us still.

Our Personality Type

A few years back, while I was an undergraduate student, my interpersonal communications professor instructed the class to take the 16 Personalities quiz. In taking the quiz, we'd receive an extraordinarily accurate description of who we are and why we do things the way we do. I took the test and was described as an INTJ, an Architect personality.

I remember chuckling after reading the results. "Rational and quick-witted . . . these personalities can be both the boldest of dreamers and the bitterest of pessimists. Architects believe that, through willpower and intelligence, they can achieve even the most challenging of goals. . . . Architects, independent to the core, want to shake off other people's expectations and pursue their own ideas."[6] You may not know me personally, but from reading this book so far, can't you say that result is so me?! Well, not the pessimistic part (insert wink here), but everything else is pretty close, eh?

My results went on to say how this personality type questions everything. "Many personality types trust the status quo, relying on conventional wisdom and other people's expertise as they go about their lives. But ever-skeptical Architects prefer to make their own discoveries. In their quest to find better ways of doing things, they aren't afraid to break the rules or risk disapproval—in fact, they rather enjoy it."[7] (I definitely do.) "But as anyone with this personality type would tell you, a new idea isn't worth anything unless it actually works. Architects want to be successful, not just inventive. They bring a single-minded drive to their passion projects, applying the full force of their insight, logic, and willpower. And heaven help anyone who tries to slow them down by enforcing pointless rules or offering poorly thought-out criticism."[8]

I remember laughing out loud reading that part, and I just did so again while typing this copy into the book. Truly, I am fiercely independent; I enjoy forging my own path to the point where I will actually go the opposite way if I feel something is too similar. I embrace being a creative, but success has to stem from it. I will do my all to best inform myself and will put 100 percent of who

I am into every project I am passionate about or else I won't commit in the first place. I embrace valuable input, especially when it's needed, but if something will hinder and not help a situation, I view it as unnecessary and I will carry on.

God has even made our personalities and quirks, and it's the coolest thing how wildly different we all are. I embrace how I was created; my quirks and my personality are multifaceted and I like that. I'm not primarily driven by emotions. I value intellect and straightforward thinking more. That's not to say I am not a compassionate person. As one who is often misunderstood, I am constantly putting myself in someone else's shoes, especially when they're hurt. I take a genuine interest in trying to understand the experiences of others, and empathy is a superpower I will never forsake. I'm protective of myself, my loved ones, and those who are vulnerable. Making people feel seen matters to me.

I appreciate how I am observant, and I'm a good listener. I can be loud and boisterous with family and friends, but I am quiet in nature, and I speak when I have something to say. I notice the little things and the details that matter. I take notes and draw tentative conclusions. I can tell at first glance how someone is feeling. I watch well. And though I am open and loving, I am guarded in some ways and able to shield myself from high hopes or people letting me down.

A good friend was with me when we took the test, and we discussed our results, laughing about the parts that were true, seeking clarity from one another, and double-checking if certain things were false. In some ways, I felt the results painted me as cold and calculated, and I found myself declaring, "Hey, that's not true!" We took note of the discrepancies and refuted the parts that didn't apply to us.

There were simple things like, "Well, this can't be true because while I'm introverted, I love planning events where we can all come together." And there were more unattractive descriptions like being ever skeptical or how it's *possible* for my personality type to be both the boldest of dreamers and the bitterest of pessimists. Dreamer? True. Bitter pessimist? Far from it. Trust me, I'm all for descriptive callouts (even if undesirable) but only if they genuinely apply to me. I know myself enough to discern what is and what isn't, and I also have trusted mirrors in my family who can share what they see. It's so important to be surrounded by people who can see us for who we really are and can lovingly point out the parts that need adjustment. (It's also important to know who we are in Christ so when someone attempts to paint us in a false narrative, we don't have to accept their perspective.)

My friend and I came to the important conclusion that the test was fun, and it was great getting insight on parts of ourselves we sometimes can't explain. However, what is sometimes seen as a negative trait can be viewed as a positive when we recognize the Holy Spirit in the mix of who we are and who we are becoming. For example, being fiercely independent is naturally beautiful when I am totally dependent on God spiritually.

Not only that, with the Holy Spirit indwelling us, we make room for the Lord to get rid of or shine a light on traits that are not like God. For example, being a dreamer can be a negative if you don't get things done. However, when you bring God into the equation, being a dreamer is beautiful because faith alone causes you to believe in the impossible. A dreamer can rely on God to help execute the vision.

You and I have complexities that an online test cannot capture. Reason one is that our personal life experiences further shape us. Reason two is the Lord has created us uniquely, making the discrepancies or missing parts of these quizzes more obvious. There are categories and sub-categories and sub-subcategories within us all! There is more than what we show, and there is more than what we can see ourselves.

The Way We Are

How would you describe your personality? What are you like when you're around people? How are you when you're by yourself? What were you like as a child? Do you believe the popular idea that babies are born with a blank slate and that our environments determine who we are? Or do you believe your personality was God given?

It's not uncommon to refer to Psalm 139 as an example of how God intricately created us and knows us from the inside out. But let's sit at verse 13 for a little bit. I learned it in the NIV, which tells us God was creatively intentional in forming our "inmost being" and how we were knit together in our mother's womb. In the Message paraphrase, it sounds a little clearer with, "You shaped me first inside, then out." David, the psalmist of this passage, wasn't referring to just our organs!

Our Creator was not only intentional in masterfully painting how we would look (which is wonderfully and marvelously made, by the way) but also purposeful in putting together our inner person. Plus, He worked on that first! This shows that God was involved in the formation of our unique *personalities*, beautiful minds, strengths and shortcomings, likes and dislikes, and beyond. While our surroundings have a continuous and weighty impact on our lives, the Lord formulated us in a way that would reflect His image.

I'm always dumbfounded when I consider the works of God's hands. The world is filled with such vivacious color, variety, and beauty; the world is full of us! I was checking out the world population clock recently, and I watched the count tick higher and higher. Within seconds, there was new life. In fact, there is a net increase of one person every 0.40 seconds![9] Insane. And get this: according to Worldometer, there are almost 8 billion people alive today.[10]

But you want to know what blows my mind? The creativity of God to whip up billions of people and no two people being the same. Think of all the combinations! Yeah, I'm not into math so I won't try. But okay, think about this: we are all tailor-made, uniquely us in appearance, personality, heart, will, and mind. We are divinely special, intricately thought out and . . . it was *easy* for God to think us all up and breathe us to life. What a brilliant, all-encompassing Creator we serve.

I'll say this plainly: you are awesome. I don't need to know you to know that you are. You have something no one else can offer; you are someone no one else can be. I need you to be amazed at yourself because you are something God did. You are His best work! And as His creations, it is pivotal we flourish in the way He intended for us to. Embrace who you are. I'm all about that.

On one of the final days of the Daniel Fast, I also learned that the Lord leads us to challenge our perspectives and our personalities. I was minding my business, looking for a sermon to watch to end the fast, and I headed over to Jackie Greene's channel as I saw she was live with a session called "Thoughts TURN UP."[11] Jackie was joined by a few women who serve in her church. They gathered around a couch and opened their hearts about what God was revealing to them about their thoughts; it was a beautiful display of transparent sisterhood. God showed me some vital things about myself that I know will help you, too!

I was reminded that with my personality type, I am not one to retreat. I go after the things of God with full faith; I have big dreams, and I'm not afraid to work toward them. I am relentless with my pursuit, but that doesn't mean I won't get wary or weary. And when I do, God is aware: even the apprehensiveness and tiredness I feel matter to Him. He desires for me to shake it off and return to the me He intended me to be—the one free from the heaviness. I was reminded to believe what God says, regardless of what I see or feel right now. He has given us everything we need in this present moment, and He will fulfill His promises to us.

One woman's story was that she believes in and encourages other people, but she doesn't do the same for herself. The Lord revealed that her inability to vocalize it for herself was due to fear! She shared that she was learning that if the promise is not yet here, it's because God is still doing a work so she can get the best version, the full version. Isn't God so sweet for speaking through her like that? I was reminded that long-suffering will be rewarded with God's very best. And when another young woman confessed she had to combat the lie that things will always be this way, I was reminded that God showed me how our thoughts can be overcome, too. We are not alone in this, sis.

One of the most profound moments for me was when one woman said that in spite of the crying and disappointments, she's choosing to believe the truth. How she explained it wowed me. She shared that her flesh is not truth, and we all know that our flesh isn't. But have you ever considered how our minds are not truth either?

It's not uncommon to subconsciously include the mind, common sense, and logic and intellect in the category of truth. I know I've done it! I admire how human intellect and discernment kick in. I can recognize lies. I'm great at filtering through what's important and what's not. Of course, I know our minds have the power to deceive, but when they aren't playing tricks, isn't what they think truth? Isn't it logic? That was what I thought. But in her testimony, I learned that a crucial step to winning the war in our minds is to know what is *not* the truth. **God's Word is truth. We know this. Our minds are not truth. This is something to embrace.** Regardless of how beautiful your mind is, how much of a creative or a genius you are, or if God has given you the wisdom of King Solomon—our minds are not truth. Logic isn't synonymous with the truth. I feel like that revelation alone will free somebody!

Even the God-given parts we appreciate about ourselves can get in the way of the Lord having His way. Isn't that crazy? I can take it one step further. Have you ever given an explanation to someone for "the way you are" or why you can't change? Maybe you said, "That's just the way I am." Or maybe you used the good old "God made me this way" line. That can very much be true . . . but it can also be false and an excuse.

One woman spoke on habits God had to break. She used waking up early as an example. Are you an early bird? I'm certainly not. However, I've been finding the beauty of early mornings even if it takes a groggy version of myself a little while to see it. Anyway, the Lord showed this young woman that if she stopped making excuses for the way she is, He could show her how to wake up early. Habits form in our minds. Don't you believe God has the power to reprogram them?

We mustn't take so much pride in who we think we are that we don't give God the room to do a work and show us who we have the power to be. We mustn't hold our old selves or certain personality traits as a banner. The Lord alone is our banner.[12] When we allow Him to reign over us, when we allow Him to fly high over us, He shows us what we can do. He can train us to do anything if we are willing. He alone defines our identities—not our reasoning, not our personalities, not our logic. We are too wonderfully complex to box ourselves in like that.

Reflection Questions

1. Have you ever taken a personality assessment? If so, how well do you think the results described you? Did you gain any insights?

2. Do you struggle with thinking the logic and intellect of your mind is "truth"? If so, what can you take away from this chapter to help you remember where truth is really found?

3. How can you celebrate the reality that you are "God's best work" while remembering that not all your personality traits are in line with God's truth?

9

Fear, Friendship, and Foes

A rule I have had for years is: to treat the Lord Jesus Christ as a personal friend. His is not a creed, a mere doctrine, but it is He Himself we have.

Dwight Lyman Moody,
New Sermons, Addresses, and Prayers

Is the Lord your friend or foe? When you do something you regret, do you go to God or do you shame yourself? Do you feel as though God will meet with you only if you have been "good"? Do you try to cover up your mistakes or rack up "holy points" to win Him over? How we behave toward God reveals who we believe Him to be. What I'm really asking is, how do *you* see God?

Before the fall, Adam and Eve could see the Lord clearly; they lived in perpetual communion with their Creator. They were shamelessly naked, completely vulnerable with

God, and trusted Him effortlessly. The first inhabitants of Eden enjoyed the unhindered company of God.

When Satan approached Adam and Eve in the garden, his first words implied that they should be suspicious of God and what He said. Adam and Eve made the conscious choice to consider his suggestion and to act upon the enemy's implication. They were influenced by an evil proposition, and their one decision initiated the corruption of the heart that we are all subject to today.[1] Immediately, Adam and Eve's eyes were opened and their perspectives about themselves, the world around them, and the God they were once so intimate with changed. Realizing they were naked, they tried to cover up, and they experienced something unfamiliar: they became afraid of their Creator.

Sin makes us feel as though being vulnerable with God is not safe. It is the most obvious obstacle that separates us from Him. But John 3:16 reminds us that Jesus closed the gap, and we are reconciled when we accept Christ as our Lord and Savior. So, if it's not sin that's keeping you away, what is it?

Could it be Satan's suggestions? If we compare our contact with the enemy to Adam and Eve's, "a sobering aspect is that God shows they were fully aware of Satan when he communicated with them. However, we realize that a spirit being can communicate with a human by transferring thoughts, and the person might never know it!"[2] We often assume that these thoughts entirely originated within ourselves.

Satan would love to have you think (even subconsciously) and then act like the Lord is your enemy. That's what he did in the garden of Eden, and it is what he is trying to do in the garden of our minds now. Are your fruits choking on the pesticides he has poured? Is your soil dry and unable to produce fruit? Have you planted but fail to reap?

Our real enemy sows seeds of doubt in our garden with questions that seem innocent and sound like us. *Did God really say that? Can you really trust Him? Does He really want to hear from you? Is He actually your friend, or will He drop you at the first sight of failure? Does He have your best interest at heart, or is He keeping the best for Himself?*

Sometimes we utilize Satan's suggestions to support a misconstrued idea of what we believe the Bible says. For example (and I told you I was coming back to this), the enemy takes it to his advantage when we don't know what it means to fear God. He loves to see us shaking in our boots, awaiting swift judgment, and he laughs because our ignorance keeps us from getting closer to God. He will egg on the notion that God is too holy to deal with our hot messes. He knows that when we cower in fear before the Lord, we reject ourselves and our Savior.

The truth is, Jesus calls you friend, and when He laid down His life for you, He was demonstrating the greatest love.[3] Another truth is that we can balance fear and friendship with God. Hear me out: for those who are not saved, the fear of God refers to the judgment of God and eternal death. For believers of Christ, it's much different.

Psalm 25:14 tells us, "The LORD is a friend to those who fear him," which shows us that "God inspires at once awe and love, fear and friendship."[4] When the Lord tells us to come before Him in fear and trembling, He refers

121

to reverence. The English Standard Version of Hebrews 12:28–29 is a great depiction of this: "Therefore let us be grateful for receiving a kingdom that cannot be shaken, and thus let us offer to God acceptable worship, with reverence and awe, for our God is a consuming fire." This kind of fear is a motivating force to draw closer to our Creator.

A Healthy Admiration

We're going to go deeper in this conversation about friendship with God, but first, I'd like to share a distinction that may be helpful when referring to the fear of God. Martin Luther differentiated between a "servile fear" and a "filial fear."

Luther defined *servile fear* as the type of fear a captive has for his malicious tormentor. "It's that kind of dreadful anxiety in which someone is frightened by the clear and present danger that is represented by another person. . . . Servile refers to a posture of servitude toward a malevolent owner."[5]

On the other hand, *filial fear* refers to the honor a child has for their parent. "In this regard, Luther is thinking of a child who has tremendous respect and love for his father or mother and who dearly wants to please them. He has a fear . . . of offending the one he loves, not because he's afraid of torture or even of punishment, but rather because he's afraid of displeasing the one who is, in that child's world, the source of security and love."[6]

I think that's really helpful! It aids us in understanding Proverbs 1:7, which says, "The fear of the LORD is the beginning of knowledge."[7] My mother used to tell that to me and my siblings whenever we had any difficulty with a school assignment. R. C. Sproul says, "Until we understand who God is and develop a reverential fear of Him, we cannot have true wisdom. True wisdom comes only from understanding who God is and that He is holy, just, and righteous."[8] Mama was right.

Again, the focal point in filial fear is an awareness of awe for the supremacy of God. While we are called His friends and have the privilege of calling Him Father, we're to always sustain a healthy reverence and admiration for Him. Going further, it is wise to maintain a component of the understanding that God *can* be frightening. Hebrews 10:31 says, "It is a terrible thing to fall into the hands of the living God." Yes, the Lord judges from the lens of love and righteousness, but as sinners, part of our motivation for reconciling with God is the fear of His judgment. I like how one writer tells it: "Fearing God means having such a reverence for Him that it has a great impact on the way we live our lives."[9] We understand that the Lord is on our side when we have a full understanding of what it means to fear Him.

Heart of Worship

In overcoming the battle of the mind, it's important we realize not only the truth of who God is but that He is on our side. God is approachable. He is welcoming. His fire entices us near. I love how Jewish ethicist Abraham Heschel once said, "Awe, unlike fear, does not make us shrink from the awe-inspiring object, but, on the contrary, draws us near to it."[10] That sounds familiar, doesn't it? That's because the very idea of God calls us to worship!

Worship is not synonymous with music. It's not filling up the silence or having the band play a couple of tunes before the sermon. Worship is not just a song, the words you cry out, or how high you're able to lift your hands. Worship is a state of being, and God requires we do it in spirit and in truth.[11] He knows when it's done in vain!

In Matthew 15:8–9, Jesus addresses this kind of worship by saying, "These people honor me only with their words, for their hearts are so very distant from me. Their worship is nothing more than the empty traditions of men."[12] Here we see that worship means absolutely nothing if our hearts aren't being moved toward God.

What exactly does it look like to worship from the spirit and to be driven by the truth? John Piper says it best: "Right worship, good worship, pleasing worship . . . depends on a right mental grasp of the way God really is, truth. If we worship an idol of our own creation, we are not really worshiping God."[13]

Powerful.

The truest state of worship is founded on a proper acknowledgment of God's nature, and it is a proper esteem of God's worth . . . which is infinite! Can you see why the enemy will use anything (the busyness of life, strongholds, condemnation, the wrong perspective of God, etc.) to keep you from being intimate and, in turn, knowing who God really is? Do you see why hell is unleashed on your heart and confusion is inflicted in your mind to prevent you from delighting in God and finding full satisfaction in Him?

Our worship was designed to "put the supreme worth of God on display."[14] How can we do this? The Passion Translation of Romans 12:1 gives us the answer: "Beloved friends, . . . surrender yourselves to God to be his sacred, living sacrifices. And live *in* holiness, experiencing all that delights his heart. For this becomes your genuine expression of worship."

You see that? We were called friends—again! *Beloved friends.* And as His friends, God lets us in on the proper response to His marvelous mercies: "we worship God authentically when we know him truly and treasure him duly."[15] In other words, we express true worship with the right knowledge of God and when our hearts respond to that knowledge by treasuring the Lord above all else. From that place, this "deep, restful, joyful satisfaction in God overflows in demonstrable acts of praise from the lips and demonstrable acts of love in serving others for the sake of Christ."[16]

Friend, we can have the heart, mind, and spirit of true worshipers in our daily life.

Expressing the Heart Stuff

If you're my friend, and I mean my absolute truest friend, you will know the truth of what I am feeling. I discern whether or not it is my flesh at work; I'll pause and use wisdom for when I should reveal those thoughts. I definitely consider sensitivity levels. But I will speak boldly and deliver in a way that is honorable and loving. For my closest friends, I throw my entire being into it, no hiding. I take a similar approach with God, but I bring Him *every*thing and of course, it's mixed with a supersized serving of reverence.

I remember the first times my family and friends experienced the frankness of my relationship with God firsthand. My mother was almost indignant, saying, "You can't say that!" My siblings would question: "You can say that?" My best friend expressed, "I'm impressed you said that." It inspired a new way of expressing themselves with God.

To reiterate, I'm not one who is trying to see how far I can go before reaching the line of disrespecting God, and I am not encouraging you to do that. I wouldn't dedicate an entire section to fearing God if that was the case! I want to show you that if you're disinterested with where you are in life, you can tell God, your Friend, "I'm bored." If you're upset, you can tell Him, "I don't like that it happened." If you're crying, you can confess, "I feel like You hurt me."

What you're feeling is what you're feeling, but that doesn't mean it is the truth. If you're feeling iffy about this kind of blatant expression, keep in mind that a true friendship requires transparency, and faith requires belief. You can feel these things, and the Lord will still consider you righteous as you express what's on your heart. Abraham spoke out about a lot of things, and James 2:23 still tells us, "Abraham believed God, and God counted him as righteous because of his faith. He was even called the friend of God." Plus, if you read Exodus 33:12–18 in the Message paraphrase, Moses will truly show you exactly what audaciousness looks like!

I came across this quote recently and related to it so well. Martin Luther was said to "pray with the reverence of addressing God and the boldness of addressing a friend."[17] I love that—I do that! I know the freedom I feel to express myself with God stems from my personality and the fact that I fully embrace the invitation to be honest. But I also believe traumas forced this sort of expression out of me, too. I had a conversation with a good friend about the word *trauma* during the early stages of the pandemic. We defined the word, made it personal, and had an eye-opening experience when we realized where we suffered. I had never considered that it could apply to me. I thought it was solely applicable to victims of abuse.

In the past five years, God has shown me what it really means to get in touch with my emotions fully, and in doing so, I'm coming out of minimizing things that hurt. There are some wounds that I wasn't even aware of until time went on or something happened and I was like, *Whoa, what was that?* But clearly those wounds were in my heart. I just didn't know until they showed themselves.

I'll never forget the time a friend of mine and I attended a Priscilla Shirer event one summer in New York. I don't even remember what she was speaking about, but I do remember this: the "come to Jesus" part at the end. She stood on that New York stage and lovingly spoke to those who were believing for healing.

My friend and I were near the back of the room; the room was dark with only the stage lit. I watched people around me stand to get their healing as Priscilla called on their ailments one by one: healing for the body, healing on the mind, financial healing, healing within relationships, and so on. I sat there, not needing any of what she mentioned but believing in the healing for those people who did. Then Shirer shared an invitation I'd never received before. Maybe the pain you're suffering isn't physical or can't be seen on the outside. Maybe you need healing from a hurt that's unexplainable . . . the hurt of a broken heart.

Girl, that knocked the wind out of me. I never witnessed tears leave my eyes *so* fast. I wept and I wept and I wept. My friend caressed my back and held me as the nearby attendant brought me tissues. I'm tearing up even as I write this.

While I'm empathetic for others and can instantly pick up what others are feeling, I lacked empathy for myself. You see, when my people would ask me how I was doing, for a long time, I would struggle and tell them something along the lines of, "I don't know. I guess I'm okay." Or I would tell them I would let them know once I figured it out. In either scenario, I would list the things I was so happy to accomplish that day. A friend recently likened that behavior to a high-functioning addict. I am good at holding on. It didn't matter what was going on at home or in my heart, because if I could still smile and if I could get things done (and done with excellence), then I was good.

When it came to considering the person suffering from a physical ailment or any sickness, I would find their pain as most important. I saw that type of ailment as one that required immediate attention. I knew all too well what that was like by seeing what my mother suffers firsthand. But I didn't know I was weighing outward pain more than the hurt I carried in my heart. I did not know that this whole time, I was telling my heart, "You can wait." I didn't know I was telling it, "You'll be fine." I didn't know I was telling it, "There are bigger issues." As I sat in that seat, God showed me that time doesn't heal wounds; He does.

And I was someone in great need of that healing power. Yes, my heart needed immediate attention, too.

Have you ever felt an emotional pain so deep you begin to feel it physically? That's what happened after my first serious breakup. I lost my appetite and several pounds and yet was doing my best work. I know it was God who kept me, and I am proud of myself for how I flourished in that season, but looking back, I'm seeing something for the first time. My work and travels were a welcome distraction, of course, but they also sort of blinded me.

Since that Priscilla Shirer event, it's been a journey of the Lord validating feelings I didn't know mattered. When I was betrayed, He told me, "I saw that." When I was sleep-deprived and frustrated that my mother wasn't healed, He assured me that He cares about my lack of sleep, and He loves how I love her, but He loves her best. As the eldest daughter, I still have difficulty showing my sensitive side at times. And I'm still a friend who sometimes shies away from the "gushy stuff." However, I've come a long way from being the girl who barely cried, and only then in private.

Now you know why when something shows up within me, I have to share with God. It's not good to let it fester in my heart; I'd rather address it with my Friend. I'll confess with tears blurring my eyes, mascara running down my face, or my falsies falling off. It's happened, you guys—and in public! Freedom within true friendship makes you not care.

Your Special Connection

One of the things I've told God is, "You let everyone hurt me!" I shifted away from this thought with the truth that

God isn't against me. But I still think it's extremely important to feel. That's why we were given emotions! The Lord has allowed me to express my hurts and cleansed my soul with weeping until I really was okay. Currently, one of the enemy's attacks is to make me believe that God is happy to see me in pain.

Remember when I shared my salvation testimony in the beginning? Fear drew me to religion, but God's love drew me to Christ. When I realized I was seeing God the wrong way (a ruthless Judge), the Lord began to show me how I could shift my perspective. I began to learn the names of God for myself, but most importantly, I learned who my Friend is through intimate encounters.

He affirms me when I feel rejected; He comforts me as I cry; He reveals Himself to me when I embrace Him; He answers me when I have questions; He rebukes me when I am wrong; and He draws me close in His love. There have been moments when I felt like my heart would explode with the overwhelming feelings I have for Him. Even as I write to you now, I think about how it's impossible to explain the depth of my relationship with the One who has been rescuing me over and over again. Truly, only the two of us could ever know. True intimacy with God is when you feel it's just the two of you even if you're in a crowded room. No one can fully understand your relationship with God because intimacy with God is *personal*.

But wait: I know what it's like to be in a church full of congregants having their own encounters and wondering why I haven't been hit the same way. Maybe you thought those Christians were "deeper" than you are, or maybe you went my route and thought something was wrong with you because you were not experiencing God the way they were. Friend, I want to free you with this thought: a great thing about our God is that He can tend to *all* His friends at once. He won't leave you feeling rejected. He will affirm you with His love and attention.

And also remember this: your special personality was given to uniquely connect you to your Creator. Because we were all made distinctively, we're all going to experience Him in distinctive ways. Get this: there are different styles of interacting with God. You can be an enthusiast, a naturalist, a sensate, an activist, a traditionalist, a caregiver, an intellectual, a contemplative, or an ascetic.[18] You're likely a combination of a few. When you grasp how our Creator has wired you, you'll enjoy the process of exploring your relationship with Him even more.

Oh, and one last thing: intimacy with God is available to you. The best way to get to know God is through personal experience; it's finding your way back to the garden and simultaneously back to Him. Intimacy with God is the weed-whacking, soil-replenishing, crop-enhancing tool we need for the garden of our mind, spirit, and soul to flourish. Getting to know who God is isn't a risk. It's a great reward. It all comes down to trust; we can't be intimate with someone we don't trust.

God Is Close

To create a lasting shift in our minds, it's important we realize the truth of who God is, the reality that He is on our side. Now, we'll discuss that He is also *by* our side. Intimacy occurs when you allow yourself to be fully known and loved by someone. At the heart of intimacy is trust. We determine how much of ourselves we will share, and when we allow someone supreme access, it's because we trust them enough to allow them to know us in depth. Due to this closeness, we feel the freedom to be ourselves. Now, if a circumstance hinders that shared intimacy, we feel distant. When it comes to intimacy with God, we feel distance because of an interruption in trust, such as that caused by sin or disappointment. We've experienced both of those!

Truly, regardless of your ability to voice it, we've all felt let down by God. The good thing is, that experience births an opportunity for miracles and for friendships to deepen. Martha and Mary questioning the whereabouts of Jesus when their brother died is a perfect example of this. Charles Stanley says it like this: "Don't let your disappointment shape your view of God. Instead, rely on what you know to be true of Him."[19]

Nearness to God doesn't depend totally on learning as much about the things of God as you can. Yes, it is important to grow in knowledge if we want to intimately know God. Jesus tells us that knowing the truth will set us free.[20] And He also spoke about how people worship what they don't even know.[21] However, biblical knowledge isn't relationship; it's just religion.

What you know about a person doesn't make you close to them; you also need engagement and personal experiences. Think about it: you can know so much about a celebrity, go to all of their concerts when they're in your city, listen to their interviews, study their speeches, and support their music, but that doesn't mean you're intimate with them. Author Jon Bloom says, "Biblical knowledge is far better than gold when it fuels our trust in God, because it fuels our intimacy with God. But when biblical knowledge replaces our trust in God, it only fuels our pride."[22] Nearness to God doesn't depend on location. You can be in your bedroom, on a walk, in your workplace, or at a restaurant, and He is there. God doesn't just stay within the walls of a church building. He isn't found in revivals alone. He is the omnipresent (present everywhere simultaneously) God and draws near to you when you draw near to Him.[23]

While we may understand God is close and that He desires to be in fellowship with us, it can be difficult to feel that because we can't see Him. It's also hard when you understand that He is near, but you don't fully believe it. However, this intimacy is the hope we hold on to as believers, and it is pivotal we do not give up on it.

Reflection Questions

1. Do you consider God an intimate friend? Why or why not?
2. Friendship requires two participants. In what ways are you an intimate friend to God? In what areas do you need to improve? (When reflecting on this question, think about whether you embrace the true nature of God.)
3. Have you revoked God's access to you? Were you holding a grudge without realizing it? Have you been distant, or does He feel distant to you?

4. Letting Jesus into your heart and accepting Him as your personal Savior is only the first step. Will you let God into your heart to reign there, bringing Him your insecurities, fears, doubts, and all that you feel? Will you bring Him your hurt and pain so you can heal?

10

Don't Forget Your Helmet

But let us who live in the light be clearheaded, protected
by the armor of faith and love, and wearing as our helmet
the confidence of our salvation.

1 Thessalonians 5:8

Have you ever felt like God hinted at something exciting
for you to do, and you were a bit shocked because it was
something you've always wanted to do, so you didn't fully
believe it until you received confirmation? Same. During
the first few days of the Daniel Fast, God nudged at me
through a podcast episode. The first episode of Shawn
Bolz's *Exploring the Prophetic* podcast I listened to featured Kristen Dalton Wolfe, former Miss USA and also
my first endorser for *Claim Your Crown*.

We didn't know one another when I reached out to
her, but after coming across her work, I saw her heart for
Christ and empowering God's daughters. I knew I needed

to make the ask. She enthusiastically said yes, read the book, and gave the endorsement. We exchanged a couple of emails, but we didn't have a relationship. Fast-forward to almost a year later, and I was drawn to that podcast episode.

Hers was the most recent episode. It was as if it were beckoning me from the top of the list. I sat in amazement, thinking it crazy how much I related to her pageant testimony. And I also thought, "What's the deal with that, Lord? Why am I coming across this now?"

Only God knew of my genuine desire to do one last pageant, but when COVID hit, I doubted that was His will. I didn't even think about it anymore. As Kristen spoke, I thought about how I am a spokesperson for Haiti, a champion for women, and I felt like God was going to use me by way of pageantry one last time. But I was at a point where I didn't want to pursue a passion just because God allowed me; I wanted to do it only if I was instructed to. A few weeks later, I received numerous confirmations and was left in wonder at the creative ways in which God reveals a thing.

After receiving the confirmation, I needed someone to talk to, specifically someone who would be able to understand my situation and provide faith-based advice for a seemingly "secular" aspiration. Kristen came to mind. I went on her Instagram and asked God if He wanted me to connect with her. As I scrolled, I was reminded of her consulting brand, Trained to Reign.

I saw a photo that quite literally stopped my scrolling finger in its tracks. Kristen was smiling and glowing (seriously, the photo was shining) as she held the biggest Bible

I've ever seen. God was making it so obvious; it almost felt like He was saying, *Yes, yes, this is who you need to speak to!* Going further, the caption sealed the deal: she wrote about how her coaching is rooted in kingdom strategies and ended with 1 Timothy 4:8: "Physical training is good, but training for godliness is much better, promising benefits in this life and in the life to come."

It was perfect! How I look onstage was not my concern, and I wasn't searching for someone to teach me how to carry myself. I know who I am, and I know my capabilities. I saw this pageant as an assignment, one where I would need to armor up, and I needed someone who would give me insight on how to train spiritually. I needed strategy. I immediately signed up for a one-on-one coaching session with Kristen and get this: the session was called "Reveal."

Kristen and I met on FaceTime for the first time, and in our call together, I shared my heart for Christ and for women, the rejection and betrayals experienced, the story of how God revealed the instruction to participate in another pageant, how she came to mind, the impending spiritual warfare, and how winning was redefined for me through my past pageant experiences. I don't need a physical crown when I have a spiritual one. But also, winning to me is when I say yes to God. There's absolutely no way I could "lose" in this pageant when my will and the outcome were surrendered to Him.

Considering where I was in my spiritual walk and the atypical nature of why I was doing the pageant, Kristen took a different approach with me. We came up with a battle plan together. I'm not sure if that's what she calls it, but that's what I'm considering it! And it all began with participating in a "listening prayer." I'd never heard of that before.

Kristen told me she would lead me in prayer and guide me by setting up a few scenarios and asking me a few questions. She instructed me to close my eyes and lie in bed. I waited. One of the questions she asked had to deal with going off to battle, or in my case, the pageant. "What is the first piece of armor Jesus places on you?" she asked. Eyes closed, a picture formed before me. The title of this chapter totally gave it away, but yes, I saw a helmet!

We discussed everything I saw throughout the entire activity, but that's for another book and another time! I told Kristen about the helmet and how to me it symbolized the guarding of my mind and putting on a new mindset. I told her what God revealed to me about my thoughts during my Daniel Fast just a couple of weeks prior and how He would like to renew my mind.

Still, I had a question as I recalled how the Bible refers to the helmet ultimately representing salvation. While I knew the word *helmet* alone was reminding me that God's power is impenetrable and how we're covered because we're saved, I felt like I had to do a study to find where the concept of the helmet of salvation connects to what it means to transform our thinking.

The full armor of God is found in Ephesians 6:10–18. Essentially, we are instructed to put on the full armor of God because we're at war—not with the people we can see but "against evil rulers and authorities of the unseen world, against mighty powers in this dark world, and against evil spirits in the heavenly places."[1] The apostle

Paul goes into detail about every piece of armor and what it signifies. In those times, soldiers put on the helmet last before going off to battle, but in my season, God showed me how to put my helmet on first. Hence why we're here. When we think of the head, especially through the lens of Scripture, it is often symbolic. For blessings, hands are placed on our heads, and when cursed, the curse falls on the person's head.[2] When Jesus conquered the grave, He crushed the head of the serpent and gave us victory. When the apostle Paul tells us to put on the helmet of salvation, he is urging us to put on the protection that enables us to crush the head of the serpent, too. The helmet of salvation allows us to win our greatest battles.

As a reminder, salvation is a one-time occurrence and is a shield that comes directly from the Lord. The helmet of salvation serves as a *daily* defense and deliverance from our corrupt nature and the enemy's schemes. When the apostle Paul tells us to put it on, he is referring to the "confidence of our salvation"[3] or the helmet of the "hope of salvation."[4] Therefore, when we put on our helmet, we put on confidence or hope. We put on Jesus, or the mind of Christ. With the mind of Christ, what we see and hear checks out through the lens of Scripture. Your thoughts have no authority over you; your thoughts are *your* captives. With the power of God, you become the captor.

The helmet of salvation also gives us confidence for a better future. It provides a positive outlook and a winning mentality. Jesus promised to give us life more abundantly, and He wasn't just referring to heaven. You can have abundant life right now, so I have a question: Did you put hope on today?

Doubt versus Unbelief

Intimacy with God will show you who He is, who you are (we'll discuss more of this later), and how to put on the armor of God. Though we are precious daughters of the King, we still need to get dressed to go off to war every day. The difference is that our helmet of salvation allows us to do so from a victorious standpoint. Life shows us there will be casualties, but our crowns double as helmets and demonstrate that we are not only royalty, but we are also more than conquerors.

A potential wound can come through a robust blow of doubt. We know that the enemy comes to steal, kill, and destroy, and our minds are one of his primary targets. He throws grenades of discontent and dangerous comparisons that explode before us; bombs full of lies land right at our feet, and the fog makes it difficult to focus on anything but momentary things. However, with the helmet of salvation, we can know there is a faithful way to deal with the attacks, including the way we express our doubts to God. Contrary to popular belief, God welcomes our doubt.

The Bible demonstrates time and time again that God embraces people who doubt. There is a difference between asking Jesus questions in an attempt to ensnare Him (the Pharisees exemplify this) and asking Jesus questions because you desire to understand. Remember, Peter began to sink when fear gripped him as he walked to Jesus on the tumultuous waves of the storm,[5] and yet Jesus reached out to him. Mary asked how she could give birth if she was a virgin,[6] and the angel provided the answer she needed to embrace what was to come. Abraham chuckled when God told him he would be the father of nations when Sarah was way past the age of childbearing,[7] yet here we are today.

The name "doubting Thomas" refers to the lack of belief that Thomas, one of Jesus's twelve apostles, displayed when the other disciples told him Jesus appeared to them after the resurrection.[8] Thomas basically said, "I'll believe it when I see it." He desired to put his hand where the holes of the nails were. I respect Thomas for this, don't you? All he wanted was to see for himself! He wanted to experience what the other disciples experienced: an intimate encounter. And Jesus, being the sweet Savior He is, showed up just for Thomas. He will show up just for you.

It's common to confuse the two, but there is a difference between doubt and unbelief. British evangelist and author G. Campbell Morgan once said, "Unbelief is an act of the will, while doubt is born out of a troubled mind and a broken heart."[9] Does that sound like you? I want to dispel any fears you may have by letting you know that you are not any less of a Christian when you doubt. In fact, doubt actually displays that you are a believer! "Doubt is not the absence of faith; doubt is the questioning of faith. You can only doubt what you already believe."[10] Doubt is an obstacle we will face over and over in this life. It's not a "you issue"; it's a mind issue. Doubt is simply an attempt to grasp what God is doing and why He is doing it. Greg Laurie, pastor of Harvest Church, says, "Sometimes we need to go through the foyer of doubt to get into the sanctuary of certainty."[11]

On the flip side, unbelief is the rejection of the truth. It is not a matter of the mind but a matter of the will.

It's having heard the truth and making a choice not to believe; it's a resolute refusal. "Unbelief involves spiritual blindness and a determined resistance to God."[12] "Doubt is a struggle faced by the believer. Unbelief is a condition of the unbeliever."[13] That's not to say the enemy won't try to attack us with the spirit of unbelief, but it doesn't change the fact that it is a choice to believe the lies he spews.

Our walk with Christ wouldn't be faith if we didn't have questions. Deuteronomy 29:29 says, "The LORD our God has secrets known to no one. We are not accountable for them, but we and our children are accountable forever for all that he has revealed to us, so that we may obey all the terms of these instructions." In other words, the things that God has shared with us are what make faith possible, and the parts He keeps secret are what make faith indispensable. We know in part, because we walk by faith and not by sight. And in this crazy world of ours, why wouldn't you ask God questions?!

In honesty and humility, we can take all of our questions to Him. I love David because he was not afraid to ask God questions at his weakest state. He asked in Psalm 22, "Why have you forsaken me?"[14] You're not accusing God when you speak from that place. Writer Colin Smith says, "Just as it's part of Christian *faith* to say we know what God has revealed, it is part of Christian *humility* to say we do not know what God has kept secret."[15]

When we face doubt with our helmets fastened, we can focus on what we know of God's character. The best way to do this is by growing in intimacy with Him. He will show you how He can use what the enemy meant to be evil for your good instead. And your doubts are good when they bring you closer to the Father.

When faced with doubt, feel free to ask trusted and mature believers questions, too. God gives us community for a reason. May we constantly push one another to Christ! He cares that we are not alone in our thoughts.

God also cares about our uncertainties in the same way He cares about our times of courage. The Lord welcomes our doubts because He desires for the real you to get to experience the real Him. As we go through life, undoubtedly with questions, we can trust that He blankets us with His mysterious love day after day.

Armor Up

Without our helmets of salvation, we leave ourselves exposed on the spiritual battlefield and susceptible to deep wounds. When we do wear them, our minds are more fortified against the suggestions, temptations, and booby traps the enemy sets for us. We can choose to guard our minds from satanic influence and put on hope. With our helmets fastened and secure, we can surrender our doubts to God. He promised that once we put out trust in Him, He will save us. We must rejuvenate our minds by meditating on the truth of God, praying, and praising in all circumstances.

Because of the helmet of salvation, we can pray for the Holy Spirit to illuminate and activate our heavenly mind. We can quiet our mind and adopt the peace that surpasses all understanding. We can shift our thoughts to whatever is true, noble, pure, lovely, and admirable. We can filter through what's real and what is not. Our minds can bow to Philippians 4:6–9, where we are told not to worry but to pray about everything. We can shift our minds to the techniques God has given us. Every day of our lives is a war, and we need to be dressed from head to toe in the armor He has provided.

Let's go back to that listening prayer: when I was fully dressed in the armor God gave me, I asked Him what it all meant. I envisioned myself in glittery metals. The armor fit, but it was heavy, and it made a lot of noise. I smiled as I thought of the inspiration behind the brand God led me to create years ago: Adorned in Armor.

Launched in 2013 as the armory for the slaying fashionista, the cutting-edge creative, and the bold believer, Adorned in Armor serves as a source of killer inspiration and encouragement toward their audacious dreams. I was inspired by Ephesians 6, and since I'm a fashionista, I thought of the passage in terms of clothes, too! I share how to get dressed spiritually and physically in order to fight victoriously.

God later led me to create *Dressed for Battle*, a podcast that serves as a reminder of the victory you have over anything that flies your way. It will remind you that you are protected and loved even when you are feeling your lowest. It will remind you that there is more to our existence—this material life isn't the only life.

I named it *Dressed for Battle* since that's already the tagline of Adorned in Armor. On the show, I interview millennial and Gen Z women of faith to discuss the struggles we're currently dealing with. So many times, we focus on success stories and the breakthrough at the end of the pain. But I want to share the stories of those who have a testimony in the making. I share the weapons and armor we could use to fight back in the middle of the battle.

Kristen gasped when she heard the backstory and totally forgot my Instagram handle at the time was @adorned inarmor. She, too, saw me in an armored dress! I will say to you what she told me: "You better clink around! Let those demon spirits know that you are present!" And I'll also add, let the enemy know that *you* know that through God, you've won. As you dress every morning, keep in mind it's not just your body that needs adornment. Your spirit needs it, too.

Reflection Questions

1. What doubts do you need to bring to God today?
2. How can you envision your helmet protecting you?
3. How can you put on hope in the face of discouraging situations?

PART 3

CROWNED

11

The Gift

We often don't realize that where God puts us is the very
place we need to be to receive what He wants to give us.

Priscilla Shirer

Let's set the scene again, shall we? It's still October 2020,
my Daniel Fast is over, and we're about a week away from
my birthday. My sister Medgina burst into my room expressing her frustration with her inability to find me the
perfect birthday present. She explained how I am the
"hardest person" to get a gift for because I am the "least
materialistic person" she knows. It's true I love gifts (who
doesn't?), but the ones I treasure most are unique in nature
and typically ones I can make great use of. She finished
off with saying, "I haven't seen you jump for joy over a
present in a long time."

I smiled as she spoke and also recalled a word that was shared with me the week before at the first in-person church service I'd attended since the pandemic began. It was right after my Daniel Fast ended; I was sitting in a crowd of people when a minister told everyone with a birthday in the month of October to come to the altar. He waited as a few of us went up, then he prayed. When he landed on me, he announced, "You will receive the best gift this month." I hadn't shared that moment with Medgina, so her observation made me chuckle. I mused inwardly: *Lord, I am waiting. Only You can fulfill my wants and needs.* Truly, I had no idea what in the world could make me jump for joy, but I knew God alone would supernaturally provide it.

In the meantime, I was in the process of figuring out how I could celebrate my birthday in a pandemic. The spa sounded great. I had been wanting to experience this extremely popular establishment I kept seeing on Instagram, so I did my research, sent out my invitations, and prepared to book a day pass when the funniest thing happened. I opened my email to find that a luxurious Christian spa two towns over had reached out to me for a paid collaboration. I no longer had to travel an hour or pay to treat myself for my birthday. God treated me! Not only did I have an all-inclusive experience, but I was *compensated* and was allowed three guests to join me. Talk about favor! The previous year, God hooked me up with an all-expenses-paid trip to a resort in Mexico, but that's a whole testimony of its own! (P.S. I did receive the best gift in 2020, and I'm not referring to the spa! It's one money couldn't buy, a gift that I'm keeping between me and God.)

I just love how attentive God is to us. He sees what matters to us, He doesn't downplay it, and He desires to give us presents that will put a smile on our faces and in our spirits. But not only that, He miraculously provides us opportunities to practice new levels of gratitude and to be awestruck by His sweet goodness. My experience with God always draws me back to the fact that He is a loving Father who caters to me. I have no idea how often I've said, "Thank You for being so considerate of me, Lord."

He is so mindful of you. Psalm 8:4–5 says, "What are mere mortals that you should think about them, human beings that you should care for them? Yet you made them only a little lower than God and crowned them with glory and honor." Let that sink in, sis! We are crowned with glory *and* honor.

Because I strongly believe in our royal stature, it genuinely unsettles me when I hear believers saying things like, "I'm worthless but the Lord finds me worthy," or even that common church phrase that goes, "I'm a nobody trying to tell everybody about Somebody." It sounds innocent, I know. I understand what most mean when they say this. And I totally agree we are no better than others, but what we are *not* is dirt. You are *not* a nobody. You are favored.

Many misunderstand that when David—aka the same guy who just told us we were made a little lower than God and are crowned with glory and honor—called himself "a worm" in Psalm 22:6, he was referring to how he was being treated. He pens how he was "scorned and despised by all" and felt abandoned by God. He was in such a humiliating situation that he felt like he was a despicable object and not worth any regard.

This psalm also serves as a prophecy about our Savior.[1] Jesus was rejected by His own people and wasn't welcomed in His own town. The Jewish religious leaders and Roman law enforcement detested Him; He was abhorred by a nation. He was a worm to them. David and Jesus were reproached by men; they weren't reproached by themselves! Though Jesus was treated as "less than," He *knew* He was the King of Kings.

It's time to abandon the mentality that we are nothing. We must stop referring to ourselves as "less than" and recognize our status as daughters of the King. A "woe is me" attitude is a form of false humility. It is not false humility in the sense of pride, however. Under the guise of these thoughts and sayings often lies a sense of low self-worth. But God redeems *and* esteems us. We. Are. Crowned.

A commenter on one of my videos in my royal identity YouTube playlist once said that I should repent because Christians can't be queens. But here's what I believe. First Peter 2:9 tells us we are a chosen people and royal priests. I cited Ephesians 1:11 that tells us we have "received an inheritance from God" and Ephesians 2:6 that tells us we are seated with Christ in heavenly places. I talked about being adopted into the royal family of God. There are so many harmful beliefs we submit to just because they look like humility.

The poverty mentality is one of them. That's when you feel like your resources are scarce, and you live in fear of what you can lose. It's committing to living meagerly because you find limits all around you, and the belief that someone else's blessings chip away at what could have been or should have been provided for you.

The poverty mentality can also be expressed through the boast that we as Christians *should* have nothing. Another time, an older woman commented on one of my videos, telling me to rinse my mouth with bleach before speaking of the holiness of Jesus, that He doesn't need influencers such as myself, but true disciples. The commenter expressed that I was a liar and should shut up since I have not left all my possessions to follow Christ. And there were dozens of emojis at the end of the comment for emphasis!

There are those who believe the rich won't enter the gates of heaven. They refer to Matthew 19:21, where Jesus tells the wealthy, young man to give away all of his possessions and follow Christ. Later in Matthew 19:23, Jesus tells His disciples that it's hard for the rich to enter heaven. Here, He demonstrates how the wealthy have a difficult time humbling themselves and expressing their need for God, as opposed to those who have less or are poor. It's hard for the rich to inherit the kingdom because of humility; it's not about their possessions but their hearts. Same thing applies for those dependent on their smarts, level of attractiveness, or any other attribute instead of being reliant on God.

Many argue Matthew 5:3 as grounds for why the rich can't get into heaven, too. However, when Jesus said, "Blessed are the poor in spirit,"[2] He was referring to how the *humble* will inherit the kingdom of God. This has nothing to do with wealth. Some also misquote 1 Timothy 6:10 and say, "Money is the root of all evil," but Scripture says, "The love of money is a root of all kinds of evil." Greed is evil, not money.

I do not believe in the prosperity gospel, but I do believe that God intends for us to flourish even here. There are blessings He has in store for us both on earth and in heaven. Jesus came so that we may have life in its fullness until we overflow![3] So tell me, sis, what do we look like living with a pauper mentality?! It's time to come out of the mindset that we have just enough to get by. It doesn't make sense for us, the heirs of Christ, palace dwellers, to be living through this life fearful of how we will provide for ourselves. This belief holds us back from receiving all of the treasures God has in store for us.

A poverty mentality can seriously compromise your journey with Christ. It's enslaving and wrong and isn't just adopted amongst those who lack financial resources. A poverty perspective can also exist amongst the wealthy. One writer defines it as "the mindset that believes one is inferior in quality, inadequate in capability, a magnet for failure, and lacking in resources."[4]

When you are given a gift or compensated for work, do you ever feel like you're not worth it? When you consider the gifts and talents God has given you, do you think you are too inadequate to use them? Are you hesitant with tithing because you believe you won't have enough? Do you find yourself saying or doing something along the lines of, "You know what, I'm just going to scroll on Instagram, go on a Netflix binge, and/or do some online shopping when scenes get boring. God will work things out for my good. He's in control, after all."

That's a poverty mindset, too! It can also look like the belief that there's absolutely nothing we can do about our situation. It breeds hopelessness and thrives on victimization. It's so disastrous because it places us in the role of helplessness *and* comfortability. We don't have to take responsibility when we believe we have the luxury of sitting back as spectators—even if miserable—to our destinies.

The wise principles of Proverbs demonstrate the power of discipline, diligence, sowing, and reaping and show us how to lead prosperous lives. But the enemy will have you think that less is more. He'll play the blame game with you so you're always faulting someone or something for why your life is the way it is. He'll lead you to justify your life away and have you thinking you're too spiritual to be bothered with money. Or, he'll convince you that money is not of God. He'll spur complaints so while you're going on about everything that is wrong with your life, more disasters head your way. He'll do anything to hold you back from God's best.

Maybe you fear using what you have because you don't want to ruin it or desire to save it for the most special moment even if that moment never comes. Maybe you're anxious about lacking or losing your belongings so you don't share. Constant worry and anxiety about lack or loss is a sure sign of the poverty mentality.

Insecurities are also a telling sign. Do you find yourself jealous of what other people have? Whether you are insecure about yourself because of their looks, popularity, gifts, community, or belongings, your confidence is not on good ground.

And as mentioned, negative or low self-perception is an obvious sign of the pauper mindset. Do you believe you're meant to live a life full of suffering, that you're a failure and you will never amount to anything? If you don't value yourself the way God values you or if you see yourself from a worldly perspective, surely you are suffering from the pauper mentality.

Many of us have adopted the pauper mentality even with our crowns on. May we not be like the "servant who becomes king" in Proverbs 30:21–22.[5] Scripture mentions how terrifying it is for the world to be in the hands of one who does not comprehend or honor the responsibilities that come along with being a royal. When we are ignorant of the power of our Father and the identity He gives us, we leave room for the enemy to feed us lies about what we deserve.

There's a thought from *Claim Your Crown* that often comes to mind, especially if the enemy attempts to throw lack in my face: "As heiresses to the kingdom, we must confidently come to the throne. You are not a peasant— begging God for porridge is like praying for crumbs. Whether you pray with wild faith or faith the size of a mustard seed, God desires to present a feast to His princess."[6]

Truly, when we've fully understood in the depths of our minds and hearts that we are daughters of the Most High King, we can then behave as children who know their Father can and will provide for every single need and God-led desire. In fact, our Father and King supersedes all of our expectations, and when following royal protocol, we have access to asking our Father for anything.

The Truth about Who You Are

How do you feel about titles? I used to be a fan of them because it made things a bit easier for me whenever people asked what my profession was. And of course, knowing my titles came in handy for creating Instagram bios.

I was known as the Christian girl who's the fashion influencer turned *Teen Vogue* writer turned pageant queen turned Syracuse alum turned author. But then God placed me in a season of uncertainty when I didn't know who I was. Or rather, I didn't quite know what to call myself. I would think to myself, *I'm an author, but I do more than just write. I am a speaker, but I don't do it all the time. I'm a business owner, but it's also a ministry.* I had so many *buts*, and in that silent season of working but waiting, I was so confused with who He would have me be. (Now, I wrap everything up in a bow under the title of multi-hyphenate. It especially helps in professional settings!)

As I was growing up, I found it difficult to put what I feel God has called me to do into words, and He always reminded me there is a place for me that has not yet been created. And in that tumultuous time in 2020, He cut off all titles and reminded me there is more than what I call myself. And there is more for you, too. We don't need a name to define what we do. There is a spiritual title that defines who we are.

Maybe, like me, you don't know what category you fit in. Or maybe you have names for yourself that aren't so kind and loving toward yourself. I know of a name that will eradicate every lie the world has used to warp your mind—a title that will annihilate every negative name you have claimed for yourself: daughter of God. I encourage you to study Ephesians 1:3–14, as it best reveals ten truths about being a daughter of God. You are blessed, chosen, holy, blameless, adopted, redeemed, forgiven, included, marked, and full of hope! Here's a brief overview that'll remind you to readjust your crown:

1. You are blessed.

According to the first verse, we see that God, the Father of our Lord Jesus Christ, is the one who has blessed us in the heavenly realms with *every* spiritual blessing. We receive each and every single blessing in Christ alone. What's so amazing about the blessings God bestows on us is the fact that we don't have to strive for them. They're already ours. Our inheritance has been promised to those who love Christ.[7]

2. You are chosen.

Because you are chosen, you are set apart. God sees you in a crowd of people. He looks down from His throne and knows you are one of His. God's hand on you is intentional. It's so intentional that He points out that you have nothing to do with the call on your life.

3. and 4. You are holy, and you are blameless.

To be holy and blameless are traits we gain because all our guilt was laid upon Jesus on the cross. It died there. That includes anything unholy, disgusting, shameful—every single blemish. It's no longer held against us because the righteousness of Jesus covers us. When God looks at us, He sees Jesus living on the inside.

5. You are adopted.

Jesus loves you so much that He gives you the opportunity to be free, to commune and fellowship with Him. If your earthly father has failed you in any way, know that your heavenly Father will never leave you nor forsake you. He's here to stay.

6. **You are redeemed.**

Redemption provides several benefits for the believer: eternal life,[8] forgiveness of sin,[9] a right relationship with God,[10] peace with God,[11] the Holy Spirit to live within us,[12] and adoption into God's family.[13] Titus 2:14 says Jesus "gave himself for us to redeem us from all lawlessness and to purify for himself a people for his own possession."[14] When we are redeemed, we are transformed. We are no longer slaves to sin or to fear. We are free!

7. **You are forgiven.**

When we sin and repent, God wipes our slate clean. If it wasn't for the sacrifice of Jesus, our ransom would not have been paid. Jesus paid it all, and because of that, we can break free from condemnation and live victoriously.

8. **You are included.**

God is ever so mindful of you. Not only are you included in the family of God but you're also in on one of the biggest prizes of all time: you are exposed to the truth and will inherit eternal life.

9. **You are marked.**

In biblical times, a seal was a mark indicating a letter or scroll was closed or completed. When a king or dignitary wanted to show an identifying mark with a letter, he would seal it with a resin imprint of his ring. The Holy Spirit likewise shows that believers belong to the Lord. Jesus promised us the Holy Spirit before He ascended into heaven. He calls the Holy Spirit our Comforter and Counselor. The Holy Spirit guides us. The Holy Spirit empowers us to do so much! Because no, we can't do this on our own! The fruit of the Spirit is critical. If you have accepted Christ, the Holy Spirit lives in you today.

10. **You are full of hope.**

The last verse of this Ephesians passage talks about the guarantee of our inheritance. Jesus loves us so much that He sent the Holy Spirit to be with us and to remind us we are not alone, that everything He said is true, and that though this walk with Christ is difficult, it's worth it. Our reward is in Him, and one day, we will be taken out of our suffering on this earth and revel in His glorious presence. God is not hiding His face. We have access to knowing Him, and in turn, knowing who He has called us to be.

Whether you're reading God's Word or simply going about your day, somehow, someway, the Lord will always find a special way to remind you of the precious gift of being His treasured daughter.

Reflection Questions

1. Do you struggle with believing God has the best in store for you?
2. Do you see yourself as royalty? Why or why not?
3. What is one way you will overcome a pauper mentality and shift to a kingdom mindset?

12

Biblical Affirmation

Thoughts are like a train, they'll take us somewhere. Protect by filling with the word of God.

Christine Caine

What are you thinking about right now? Probably a million things. Okay, maybe not a million but definitely a lot. In a 2020 study, researchers came up with a method to separate specific instances when a human concentrates on a sole idea; they're calling it "thought worm." They concluded that we have a new thought more than 6,000 times per day, with 6.5 thought transitions every sixty seconds![1] Can you imagine? Actually, let's not. The study didn't include calculating thought content, as experts have yet to figure how to determine the amount of negative and intrusive thoughts people typically have daily.

We don't need science to convince us there's power behind our thoughts or how our thoughts influence our lifestyle. We don't need science to know self-criticism has the power to hold us back in a multitude of ways. What we need is a solution to fight back. The world chose affirmations; I choose the Word of God.

An affirmation can be anything you say or think. Your thoughts affect the trajectory of your life. You can choose to say statements that will add to or subtract from your life. Generally, positive affirmations are effective. Imagine how much more impactful these declarations will be if they're rooted in the Word of God?! Imagine praying the promises of God over your life?!

People often say, "Just think happy thoughts" as if that's the easy solution to conquering negative thinking, but happy thoughts are situational. The only way we can have *joy and peace*, a permanent state, is when we keep our minds on Christ. You see, with positive affirmations, you are working from your own strength. With biblical affirmations, you are totally dependent on God.

The idea is simple, and yes, the act is doable—but changing your thoughts isn't easy at all. You can open your mouth and say it. True. But it's another thing to believe it. The more we say anything, the more those words start to sink in. If we start intentionally declaring the Word of God over our lives, we'll begin to believe His promises. We must be careful not to seek out affirmations rooted in worldly practices. As believers, the only thing we should be meditating on and "speaking into the atmosphere" is the Word of God.

A couple years ago, I put together what I called "biblical affirmations for queens," and it has changed lives. The free printable and video I created garnered hundreds of testimonies, as well as surprising donations to my ministry from viewers even on the other side of the globe. At the time, no one else was sharing biblical affirmations online, and when it became a trend, my lists were highly ranked on Google!

Here's some quick background as to why I thought of creating this resource. About two years ago for my celebration dinner (I know, I know there's just something about my birthday), I chose a restaurant because of the great eats, yes, but mainly because of the throne they had in the room (*hello*, photos). On a more serious note, I was going through a really rough time in my life, and I had to force myself to celebrate. That throne was symbolic of the resilience I have as a royal. It was so beautiful, and I could sense that whoever sat in that seat felt like a queen. Looking back at the photos, I was inspired to create a list about who God says we are.

Later, God did something even bigger with that idea. When I was crowned Miss Black New Jersey and was offered the opportunity to visit my homeland of Haiti with *Teen Vogue*, I was elated. I always knew God called me to minister to girls and women, but when I entered those classrooms and saw everyone enthralled with the crown, God gave me a specific mission: to remind His daughters that they have crowns that have always existed. I created the video and the free printable as a resource, and it has been such a blessing to see how much these projects have been instrumental in people's spiritual journeys.

Biblical affirmations are a staple to forming a beautiful garden around us. Remember: we create our outside world with our thoughts, so we must be mindful of what we meditate on. Dream, imagine, meditate, write down, speak aloud, sing the truth to the depths of your being! If you desire a biblical, life-transforming impact on who you are becoming, I encourage you to commit biblical affirmations to memory and declare them several times every day. We become what we believe in our hearts, after all.[2] Listen to them over and over. Share them with the royals in your life. Indeed, you will see how your negative ideations fare against the truth of God!

If you're looking in the mirror and despise what you see, Psalm 139:14 will tell you that you are God's masterpiece. If you're feeling defeated, Romans 8:31 will assure you that you are more than a conqueror. If you feel forgotten, Psalm 139:13 will tell you that you had God's attention before you were even a thought in your mother's mind.

Every single person has experienced a form of insecurity, but not everyone experiences freedom from that. The answer to such a widespread struggle is one that is extremely underrated and overlooked. Whether you've been struggling with a lack of confidence for years, it's a new struggle, or you feel like you're the most confident person in the world, here is the surefire way to love yourself in the best way possible. There is a cure that leads to contentment, and it begins with knowing your true identity.

The first weapon for guiding your emotions and overcoming the enemy by ruling your thoughts is getting to know God as Father. Another weapon is getting to know who you are through God's eyes. When you learn to see yourself in the eyes of Christ, you learn to let go of everything that blinded you to your beauty. And I'm not just talking about physical things.

Self-confidence isn't a bad thing, but it depends on . . . well, *self*. And you and I both know how hard and relentless we can be in our own minds! However, when we base our self-worth and identity on our heavenly Creator (some call this *God*fidence), we tap into some pretty powerful lenses to live out our lives.

Your identity is who you are. It's how you view yourself, and in some circles, it's how the world may view you. Your identity speaks to the characteristics that define you. It is important to get to know yourself by exploring activities, spending time alone, and cultivating relationships. However, these will provide you with only the *extensions* of yourself.

When you begin with Christ, you find your core. Indeed, He is the truest way to discovering and embracing who you are. He is the only way to living out our lives in true freedom and being who He has called us to be. God has made us so amazingly complex, and it's the coolest thing how wildly different we all are. I am not saying stop being you. I am saying, when you encounter God, you begin the process of getting to know the true you. His original design.

Second Corinthians 5:17 tells us that we become new people when we belong to Christ. "The old life is gone; a new life has begun!" We are all His creation, yes, but we become His children when we accept Christ into our hearts. When God banished Adam and Eve from Eden, it symbolized both humanity's broken relationship with God and the broken relationship between each individual and themselves—a deprivation of identity. In our separation from God, we lost our true identity. When we reinstate a relationship with our heavenly Father, He restores our identity. We become His children and we go from "in the world" to "out of it." He changes our identities by taking off the names the world calls us and instead calling us His very own.

You can begin to learn what God says about you through meditation on the Word of God. I truly believe that you can find beauty in your brokenness when you rely on God to put you back together. I also believe that learning what God says about you will empower you to start boldly refuting anything that opposes it. In fact, I'm giving you the task to begin saying, "That's a lie" out loud when you hear or believe or feel something that goes against what God says about you or Himself!

Seriously, don't you detest being lied to? And yet, we regularly listen to and even embrace the lies of Satan. When you know what God says about you, you are able to discern between His voice and the voice of the enemy. Oftentimes you won't hear a dark, sinister voice speaking evil things into your mind. Sometimes, the enemy will sound like you. That's why it's important to know what God's messages sound like and what Satan's schemes sound like. It's vital to recognize the enemy's lies to you.

I'm pinpointing every single lie of his. A couple weeks after Medgina spoke to me about finding the best gift, I discovered the reason I harbor so much anxiety about a time that's so special for me. It is an intentional cycle from the camp of the enemy. But this revelation came only after I journaled a pretty dark confession. I wrote,

I feel so dead, Father. How is my birthday approaching and I don't feel alive? How can I be living and not feel alive even with You in my life? Why can't I just fully enjoy an outing without feeling sadness? Why is the thought of my birthday making me happy and hurt at the same time? Lord, as we enter my birthday week, I pray You will be my joy, that I abide in You every moment of my life. Cover me with unfathomable peace. (October 19, 3 a.m.)

That was the weight of what I was feeling. Interestingly enough, the message preached that day by Pastor Steven Furtick was on the passage in Ezekiel 37 about dry bones coming to life. It was a sermon that awakened me for sure, especially as I was looking for Scriptures to speak to me and none felt personal in that moment. Have you ever felt that way? Like the Bible doesn't have a word for your situation? So you go through the day empty and looking for something you know only God can give, but as you wait and He doesn't seem to respond, you're on the brink of breaking.

And then someone asks you how you're doing, and unable to answer, you just burst into tears. You've composed yourself in front of your family and at work so well, but when you get home, the façade fades away. The week of the twenty-fourth, I ran errands and found my eyes watering at the most random times. I was able to blink the tears away without them falling and without people noticing, but one night when I got home and I got on a FaceTime call with a good friend, the dam broke.

It helped to have someone recognize and voice my sources of pain. It reminded me that God does that for me, and I hope this reminds you that He'll do the same for you. He will show you why you're hurting, and He will show you how to heal that wound that just seems to keep bleeding.

To overcome dark times, it's imperative to realize that though we won't hear Satan's voice or even recognize his influence in the moment, we need to shut out the voice of the enemy by prophesying to ourselves. Satan's suggestions in silence can be deafening, and when we choose to listen, we silently agree. We have to actively choose God's voice. Choose it over everything. Declare over yourself that you will live and not die. Shout, "I have what the Lord says I have. I am who the Lord says I am."

Knowing who we are doesn't make us invincible, but it empowers us to see ourselves through God's eyes, to know what He says about us, and to use that knowledge to rebuke the lies of Satan *out loud*. Yes, there is power in your voice, so don't just fight back in your head. Call the devil out! We must never accept anything that dares leave his mouth.

Prepare for the Test

Did you know that Satan knows the Bible fully? He wouldn't be so good at tripping us up if he didn't. However, he's no match for Jesus, and because Christ is in us, we are greater than Satan's tactics! That doesn't mean we shouldn't be aware, though. In Matthew 4:1–11, we learn that Satan twisted God's Word and attempted to use it against Jesus. He said to Jesus, "If you are the Son of God," do this and do that. He showed Jesus all the kingdoms of the world, telling Jesus that He could have it all if He would only bow down.

The Son of God passed the test. He not only knew the Word, He *was* the Word become flesh. He knew the mission God called Him to. He knew that by His prevailing over the enemy and conquering death, we would receive the opportunity to conquer the temptations of the enemy. He knew He had nothing to prove to Satan and instead focused on furthering the kingdom of God on heaven and earth.

The enemy will tempt you, too. He has been all along. He will say to you, "If you are the daughter of God," then do this and do that. He will use tricky language that sounds biblical, and he will try to infiltrate your mind with ungodly thoughts so that you will fail. But guess what? God doesn't shut the door and leave you alone in the test. Like a good teacher, He will wait patiently. He doesn't leave the room; He *gives* you room to meditate on how you can best respond to life's battles. He lovingly guides you to the answer: Himself.

Sometimes we may have to take the test again, but we are not penalized for it. Our previous results do not take away from the promises God has in store once we've passed. The reward is one we will obtain if we utilize the Word of God as our sword. Angels can come and minister to us when we look at our circumstances and still claim the promises of God for ourselves.

Sis, gone are the days when you struggled to lift your head up. The confidence booster we all need is Christ. When we know what God says about us, rebuke the lies from the enemy, and claim God's promises over our lives, we will experience true freedom. We will begin to see ourselves the way God intended.

Before heading off to the next chapter, I'd like to quickly address one more detrimental mindset commonly found in the community of believers: the idea that self-love and Jesus cannot coexist. It's the belief that self-love is solely a selfish act. There's a misconception that it is impossible for Christians to love God and also themselves. It's something I've run into a lot with my ministry, and I was confused by the flack.

The truth is this: when 2 Timothy 3:2 warns us about becoming lovers of self, Paul is referring to becoming absorbed with matters concerning our own interests, regardless of the welfare of the world around us. Loving ourselves in Christ does not look like that. It is possible to honor ourselves and have the desire to help others. In fact, a self-love journey in Christ leads us to do that.

A self-love journey in Christ looks like exploration—the messy kind. But it's so beautiful because it leads us to bravely face our fears and shortcomings yet choose grace, God's perspective, and to treasure ourselves anyway. This path leads us to understand that feelings are fickle and will often contradict the truth; they are not indicators by which we should see ourselves or live our lives. This journey includes allowing the Lord to show us how to deal with our insecurities and to point out when we're hiding, too. We can revel in how He affirms us in ways the world never can. We will embrace the truth that we are gifts, deserving of love—and that we should never accept anything less. In the end, we'll be forever led to the conclusion that our purpose is not just for us; it's to compel others toward Christ.

In this continual journey of loving ourselves, we will witness how there's always a fleshy issue to overcome, always a purification that needs to happen, always a hindrance that will lead us back to our dependence on God. Discovering ourselves in Him shows us how imperfect we are but how He perfectly loves and esteems us anyway. It shows us how we can prosper into our destinies as the Perfect One leads us.

So yeah, you can be confident in Christ. It is not a sin to know your worth in Him or to appreciate what He created in you. We cannot love ourselves the right way without God teaching us in the first place! And wouldn't God, the Creator of all things beautiful, want you to cherish and carry yourself with love, dignity, worth, and respect?

Reflection Questions

1. What has Satan suggested to you in silence? What lies did you choose to listen and agree to?
2. How will you actively choose God's voice today?
3. Will you allow the Lord to show you how to deal with your insecurities and to show you when you're hiding?
4. What is your favorite aspect about yourself?

13

Think like a Queen

God uses rescued people to rescue people.

Christine Caine

To think like a queen, you must know that you are one. In this chapter, I will highlight two biblical queens—Esther and Michal—who were born into or married into royalty. In both situations, these women were bred to become queens. We will look briefly at the power of their influence and how their emotions, mindsets, and/or spiritual views led them to wield their power.

I'd like to first give honorable mentions to a couple of queens who always pique my interest when I come across their names in the Bible. There is Deborah, who was not *officially* a queen but the only female judge mentioned in the Bible. She prophetically led her people to a monumental victory over their Canaanite oppressors.[1]

Then there's the Queen of Sheba. Have you heard of her?

I honestly would feel I did myself a disservice without mentioning her in this book. Maybe it's her mystery—the Bible briefly mentions her by name and provides a short account of her time challenging King Solomon.[2] I find it fascinating that the first Black biblical figure recognized for her beauty, boldness, and riches is historically known for traveling to the end of the earth to seek wisdom. What a *queen*.

While I've not found proof that the Queen of Sheba converted, some believe her return home is how Judaism was brought into Ethiopia. Luke 11:31 says this: "The queen of Sheba will stand up against this generation on judgment day and condemn it, for she came from a distant land to hear the wisdom of Solomon."

You can get lost in researching her story because you'll come across fantastical legends of Muslim and Jewish mythology, so there are a lot of blurred lines. One thing remains true in both types of sources: the biblical background. This powerful monarch was so intrigued by King Solomon's God-given wisdom that she sought it out firsthand. This leads us to ask ourselves, How far will we go to explore the depths of God? As our faith challenges us, will we go boldly before the throne of the One who unleashes wisdom and trust Him at His word? Whatever we journey through in this life, will we make the conscious choice to believe?

These next few queens will lead you to question, too.

Esther

It's impossible to mention queendom without telling the iconic story of Esther. She was a young Jew, the descendant of a severely oppressed ethnic group, and an orphan raised by her cousin Mordecai. A series of unpredictable events—including the dismissal of Queen Vashti for standing her ground (more power to ya, sis)—led Esther to participate in the world's first beauty pageant and find favor with the world's most powerful and temperamental king. More than a pauper-to-princess fairy tale, Esther is remembered as the queen who bridged the worlds of Persia and Israel.

When Mordecai uncovered Haman's plan to kill all the Jews, he asked that Esther go into the king's presence and plead for mercy. Esther would risk death by appearing before the king without being summoned. Before she followed this bold plan, she asked Mordecai to gather all the Jews in Susa to fast for her for three days. She and her attendants also fasted.

Undoubtedly, Esther was petrified. And she probably had been scared since childhood. She had suffered the loss of her parents and then was separated from her cousin after being taken away for beauty treatments that would end with her being presented before the king. Sure, she won "most beautiful" and became queen, but because of her ethnicity, she was looked down on for all of her life. While her station made her confident, there must've been moments Esther was terrified she wouldn't know how to lead, let alone be able to continue to conceal her identity from the king. She certainly felt conflicted when Mordecai came to her with disaster facing her people, but she felt she had no answer. Perhaps Esther dealt with imposter syndrome right in the palace.

Does that sound like you? Has God opened wide the door of opportunity, yet inwardly you feel unfit? Or you feel as if you're about to be found out? A question Esther could have asked is one we're all familiar with: *Why me?* She may have also wondered, *Is there a way I can avoid this confrontation?* Maybe you're at a new job and you get along with your coworkers great, but then you receive an assignment to report on something that goes against your spiritual beliefs, so you don't know what to do. Like Esther might've, are you asking God, "Why did I find favor here, and why am I the one who has to deal with this?" Or are you seeking God concerning how to deal with the situation?

Mordecai told Esther that help would arise elsewhere if she chose not to do anything about that grave situation.[3] Whether it was fear, or maybe our girl got too comfortable living a luxe life (or a combination of both), Esther's faith and love for her people is ultimately what made her a change agent. The book of Esther is the only one in the Bible that doesn't mention God, but we see the power of fasting at His feet and expecting to find an answer there. "If I perish, I perish"[4] was the queen's declaration of obedience and trust in Him.

Fasting is not the only weapon here. You are. God has already made you the solution to a problem; it is your choice to be the answer. No, it is your choice to *choose* to be the answer. Whenever you think, *Why me?*, make a list as to why it *should* be you. It is a choice to be courageous. Like the radical declaration of Esther, will you chase a word from God and choose His will over your own comfort? No matter the circumstance, may we remind ourselves that it is an honor that God chose us for such a time as this.

Michal

Oh, how my heart hurts for Queen Michal. Truly, her story reads like a Shakespearean tragedy. We are first introduced to her in 1 Samuel 14:49. She was the daughter of King Saul, Israel's first king who was insanely jealous of David, a shepherd boy turned soldier who we know as a man after God's heart and also the rightful heir to the throne.

Michal's older sister, Merab, was promised to marry David after he was enlisted to destroy King Saul's enemies in battle. David declined the king's offer. So Saul wed his eldest to a different man. Michal, 1 Samuel 18:20 tells us, was in love with David. When King Saul discovered the princess was head over heels, he then promised *her* to David but was secretly hoping David would be killed in battle. David wasn't and reaped the benefits of being married to the king's daughter. Note: the story of Michal is the only time the Bible mentions a woman loving a man first.

It looked as if things were working out in Michal's favor . . . until they weren't. Saul's jealousy got so consuming that he tried to kill David, but Michal, in her love, helped David escape. While David was on the run for his life, Michal was given away to another man. We're not told why, but it wouldn't be surprising that her father did this to Michal as punishment for aiding his enemy.

Several years later, when Michal's father had passed and David was entering into his role as king *and* situated amongst his other wives and children, he ordered his old bride to be returned to him. By force, Michal was taken back to David as her husband, Paltiel, trailed after them in tears.[5]

Can you imagine? I'm not even going to act like that order didn't subtly change my perspective of David, the biblical figure I respect most for passionately seeking God and baring his heart in Psalms. I won't judge, but let's just say . . . it made me see his humanity even more. Sure, he was a great man of God, but he was not a good man to Michal. Later on, we see how marriage to the princess was more of a conquest (as many politically positioned unions are); Michal was a pawn in a power struggle from the beginning. Bragging rights and subduing a divided nation also played a part. David referred to Michal as the daughter of Saul and himself as the son-in-law of Saul numerous times. Taking her away from the only man who had ever loved her was wrong, especially because David had no intention of loving her himself.

The next time we see Michal is in 2 Samuel 6:16–20, and y'all, sis is filled with rage. She is looking out from her window as the ark of the Lord is entering the town, and when she sees her husband dancing unlike a king before the Lord, "she despised him in her heart."[6] Ouch. Now here's the part we're more familiar with: when David returns home, ready to bless his household, Michal dishonors her husband by speaking to him in contempt and attempts to shame him for how he worshiped. The Bible shares that the couple didn't bear any children. Perhaps it was by choice or maybe it was due to how she scathingly addressed God's anointed.

Either way, this story saddens me. I feel for Michal. Still, I know the Bible is not a love story in a romantic way— everything points to the prophecy of our Messiah and how God accomplishes His plan despite the wrongdoings of His people. So why did I share the story of this royal? One writer's point answers that question: "God placed stories like Michal's in the Bible to remind us that heroes are also human and bitterness can destroy even a queen."[7]

Queen, I don't want bitterness to destroy you. Hurt and rejection are unavoidable, but bitterness—the hate and resentment that festers in our heart—is a choice. A choice that distances us from God and ultimately leads to destruction. Was Michal wrong to disrespect David? Yes. Was her hurt justified? Yes. But regardless of how much she had the right to feel her pain, there is never a reason to rob God of praise.

What better way to work toward removing bitterness from the heart than by addressing the source of it? We see Michal's bitterness was birthed from being treated like property, from experiencing unrequited love and betrayal, and from being torn away from the only man who had loved her. What is yours? When was the moment you felt your heart begin to turn? When did you feel it grow dark?

Was it because enough was enough? Truly, every woman has a breaking point, and I've been there. I spoke about some rejection and betrayals I experienced, and I mentioned how I wanted God to punish the abusers, but I didn't share with you the moment I knew something was shifting in my heart. The alarm went off (hey, Holy Spirit) when I found that I looked forward to the downfall of my enemies. That's when I knew I needed God to set my heart free.

As I was finishing this book (it's now March 2022), I watched a sermon entitled "The One Who Seeks . . . Finds!" with Pastor Steven Furtick, and he said something that I believe will really help you. He focused on the story of Ruth and Naomi, comparing the two women. While both women lost their husbands, one changed her name to "bitter" but the other chose to glean hope in the fields (both literally and spiritually). Pastor Furtick explained that when we are embittered, the devil will help us look for even more things to be hurt about and will help us harvest our hurt feelings without our needing to ask him! Furtick calls it "gleaning for garbage."[8] The devil will help you discover how people aren't trying to love you but leave you. He'll help you find the evidence as to why they left . . . which is why being selective with what you see is key. On the flip side, when we ask our Helper, the Holy Spirit, to glean treasures (hope, joy, and the gift of God), then we will receive that help.

Remember when I mentioned the power of muting earlier? In working toward my heart's freedom during the times I experienced betrayal and exclusion, I took practical steps to protect myself from any form of bitterness taking place, too. As mentioned, I had to choose to mute certain people. You'll probably go through a stage of indifference during the process. Honestly, unmuting is a pretty cool way to determine whether or not you've moved on from that hurt. Sometimes it's going to look like a constant releasing, but that doesn't mean you are not free. It just means you're human.

According to 2 Chronicles 16:9, the Lord wants to strengthen your heart! He searches the whole earth for those who are fully committed to Him. God sees how you've been treated by people, how wronged you have been, and/or the wrongs you've caused. He sees the you that you try to hide, and He knows the hurt that lies underneath it all. The best part about it is even when those closest to you have changed their perspective of you, the Lord alone knows your heart and writes your narrative. Instead of choosing bitterness and holding on to the hurt you may be justified to feel, choose a deep breath and another and another. It has been said that deep breaths are like love notes to the body. Allow the love of God to make its way through every part of you. Pause before you allow hate-inspired speech to leave your lips. Redirect your hurts into praises unto God.

Reflection Questions

1. Which queen do you relate to the most? Why?
2. Esther found fasting to be an important spiritual discipline. What situation in your life can you fast about?
3. Have you been hurt and rejected? Are you healing?
4. Has the Lord brought up a situation where you must embrace accountability? What did that look like? How will you choose to act on it?
5. What are you gleaning in this season?

CLOSING CHAPTER

The Kingdom Perspective

The human mind is the most powerful thing on earth so when you submit it to God, you become a powerful tool for the impossible.

Charles Stanley

When your world becomes more overwhelming than usual, I encourage you to look up. Our helmet allows us to filter through what is real and what's not. What's real is that you are seated in heavenly places. What's real is nobody—including Satan—can shake that. You have a heavenly citizenship; that is where our true home is. Everything we do on earth and the way we respond to everything here is laying a foundation for our promise. And usually the best way to respond—and the most powerful, life-changing way—is the opposite of what you initially feel.

Maintaining an eternal perspective is monumental for shifting our minds because the truth is that Satan wants to keep us confined in the cycles of our everyday, obsessing over everything we see on the news and social media. He wants us to believe that the walls are closing in and there's no place for us to escape. Our helmets of salvation remind us that we can come up for air and to renew our trust in the Father, who has everything under control. Kingdom-mindedness rescues us.

The kingdom was so important to Christ that He brings it up over a hundred times in the Gospels. I think it's safe to say Jesus aimed to grab our attention and was intentional in telling us where to direct our eyes! But what is the kingdom? While it is an unimaginable paradise in heaven, Jesus is the kingdom personified: and because we are His heirs, the kingdom also lives through us.

One of the verses my parents had me commit to memory as a child was Matthew 6:33. The ESV says, "But seek first the kingdom of God and his righteousness, and all these things will be added to you." In other words, put God first and watch everything fall into place. It's a very popular verse. But the context? Not so much.

When Jesus directs us to seek His kingdom first, it's within the backdrop of Him instructing us not to worry about the basics of life, such as what we'll eat, what we'll wear, where we'll live. He addresses our anxieties and temptations, and in Matthew 6:30, He tells us, "And if God cares so wonderfully for wildflowers that are here today and thrown into the fire tomorrow, he will certainly care for you." It's a mighty moment in the Sermon on the Mount, because He is making a clear distinction between what it was like living in the old covenant (under the law of Moses) as opposed to living in the new covenant (under the freedom of Jesus Christ). Life without Christ was all about striving, but the Lord invites us to a new reality that is available to us when we accept His offer to supply all of our needs and live in the abundance of His love.

What would your mind look like if you allowed God to wash away your worries and cancel out wrong thinking? He would help you apply Proverbs 4:23 and "guard your heart above all else." The mind of Christ would activate and help you screen your thoughts through the Lord's divine filter. He would show you what negative people, habits, or thoughts should be removed. There would be less entertaining of what hurts you and more of what grows you.

What would your life look like if you put the kingdom of God first? The Lord said, "All these things will be added to you,"[1] so expect to operate in purpose more! Await the provision and grace to navigate whatever goes on at school, work, or right at home. Anticipate an anointing of supernatural creativity! Activate the authority and favor the Lord has given you to walk into the rooms He has called you to walk into and sit comfortably at the tables that He has set just for you. Surely, you would have less room for fear, worries, and anxiety and would abide in Him.

Oh, but there's more. The verse tells us to seek first the kingdom of God *and* His righteousness . . . we mustn't leave out the latter! Seeking the righteousness of God shows us that Jesus wasn't just telling us to embrace the innermost reality of the kingdom but to also embrace the kingdom in the practical ways we live our lives. It's essentially saying, "Thy kingdom come, thy will be done" through our lifestyles. As we pursue the kingdom, we not only understand that life is a preview but we also bring the reality of heaven to earth by how we honor the Lord and His precepts through our daily living. How exciting is it to know that not only is the kingdom coming but we also have the God-given power to manifest the kingdom, or the will of God, right before our very eyes?!

If you're excited but still unsure of your purpose, Romans 12:2 assures us that when we allow God to transform the way we think, we will know of His will, "which is good and pleasing and perfect." When we cast aside the chase for temporary pleasures, we can look for God to answer us when we ask, "What do You want for me?" and "How can I live a life for Your ultimate purpose?" And then we can trust that we will be content with His response.

I greatly admire the apostle Paul because of how he found satisfaction regardless of where he was and irrespective of the task God had him accomplish. Even while imprisoned, suffering, and starving, he was able to have hope and be filled with courage. In Philippians 3:8, he was able to say, "I count everything as loss because of the surpassing worth of knowing Christ Jesus my Lord. For his sake I have suffered the loss of all things and count them as rubbish, in order that I may gain Christ." Paul was devoted to honoring Christ through life and death. He shows us that true fulfillment comes by perceiving the treasure.[2] Christ is His treasure. He leads us to ask, who is the king of our heart?

Matthew 6:19–21 tells us, "Don't store up treasures here on earth, where moths eat them and rust destroys them, and where thieves break in and steal. Store your treasures in heaven, where moths and rust cannot destroy, and thieves do not break in and steal. Wherever your treasure is, there the desires of your heart will also be." The treasure of Christ is a gift that will keep giving. When Christ is made king within our minds, spirits, and hearts, we obtain a prize that we win over and over again.

I recently realized something about dissatisfaction. The enemy tried to distort my view whenever emptiness tried to nag at me, but wanting more of God is always a good thing. We are held responsible when we have too little (because Christ is always available to us), but we could never have enough. I'm learning to shift my perspective away from what I feel I don't have in Him and to turn my sight to the fact that I strongly desire the Lord in the first place. I confidently reject the ideas the enemy tries to infiltrate my mind with, including those rare but random moments he pops up to try to trick me into believing that even heaven won't satisfy. I look forward to meeting the One my soul loves. I understand that Satan's tricks are a veiled perspective. Know this: whatever fears the enemy throws your way, it's to deter you from wanting God.

In this season of my life, Elevation Worship's "This Is the Kingdom" is on repeat. (I'm listening to it now as I close out this chapter.) The lyrics are literally Scripture. It's based on Matthew 6:33 and the Beatitudes, and it soothes my soul . . . probably because it speaks to a place in my mind the enemy lies to me most about. The song is a beautiful reminder that I will indeed be filled.

Queen, I encourage you to keep your eyes on the Prize. Truly, the focus of our gaze governs our measure of fulfillment, so it's imperative that we are mindful with what we're looking at. The renewal of our minds and the submission of our emotions/flesh will show us that indeed the King will satisfy us all.

As we journey through this life, may we abide in the Lord and posture our hearts to delight in Him. I pray this book serves as a resource for obtaining a winning mentality and to equip you to grow more crown-conscious every day. I dare you to release the power of the mighty, matchless kingdom of God.

Today, I pray that you will step into your royal position as the daughter of the King. I pray you discover the Lord, your God, as Father and your truest Friend. May you see and agree with His divine purposes, and may you launch forward as the empowered vessel He has called you to be and to pour from. May the Lord reveal what He desires to be dealt with, to show the ugliness of our hearts and to turn the ashes of our past into beauty. May you repent ceaselessly and experience deliverance daily. I declare that you will disrupt fear and draw a true picture of who God is.

I pray you will look forward to newfound intimacy with the Lord and that you will indeed put Him on the throne of your heart. I say yes and amen to God's promises and His will for your life. I rebuke the spirit of confusion, logic, and reasoning that tries to kill dreams. May you always ask the Lord for help. I team up with you and come against dissatisfaction and cancel out the poverty mindset so that you choose God's way of thinking.

I declare according to Psalms 16:8 that God is set before you and you will not be shaken. I pray in confidence that He will show you how to best discipline your mind and to nurture a mind of rest. I pray Romans 15:13 over you.

May God, the source of hope, fill you completely with joy and peace because you trust in him. May you overflow with confident hope through the power of the Holy Spirit.

And finally, daughter of God, may you believe, shout aloud, and walk confidently in these truths:

You are remarkably made.
> I will praise You
> because I have been remarkably and wonderfully made.
> Your works are wonderful,
> and I know this very well. (Ps. 139:14 HCSB)

You are always on God's mind.
> Oh yes, you shaped me first inside, then out;
> you formed me in my mother's womb.
> I thank you, High God—you're breathtaking!
> Body and soul, I am marvelously made!
> I worship in adoration—what a creation!
> You know me inside and out,
> you know every bone in my body;
> You know exactly how I was made, bit by bit,
> how I was sculpted from nothing into something.
> Like an open book, you watched me grow from conception to birth;
> all the stages of my life were spread out before you,
> The days of my life all prepared
> before I'd even lived one day. (Ps. 139:13–16 MSG)

You are more than a conqueror.
If God is for us, who can be against us? . . .

We are more than conquerors through him who loved us. (Rom. 8:31, 37 NIV)

You are strong and courageous.
Be strong and courageous. Do not be afraid or terrified because of them, for the LORD your God goes with you; he will never leave you nor forsake you. (Deut. 31:6 NIV)

You are not who you once were; you are forgiven.
Therefore if anyone is in Christ, *this person is* a new creation; the old things passed away; behold, new things have come. (2 Cor. 5:17 NASB)

You wholeheartedly believe your prayers are heard.
I tell you, you can pray for anything, and if you believe that you've received it, it will be yours. (Mark 11:24)

You will unashamedly live for God, not man.
I eagerly expect and hope that I will have nothing to be ashamed of. I will speak very boldly and honor Christ in my body, now as always, whether I live or die. (Phil. 1:20 GW)

You will seek first God's kingdom and His righteousness.
Seek the Kingdom of God above all else, and live righteously, and he will give you everything you need. (Matt. 6:33)

You will represent the light of Christ and shine wherever you go.
You are the salt of the earth. But what good is salt if it has lost its flavor? Can you make it salty again? It will be thrown out and trampled underfoot as worthless.

You are the light of the world—like a city on a hilltop that cannot be hidden. No one lights a lamp and then puts it under a basket. Instead, a lamp is placed on a stand, where it gives light to everyone in the house. In the same way, let your good deeds shine out for all to see, so that everyone will praise your heavenly Father. (Matt. 5:13–16)

You are covered and will find refuge under the wings of God.

He will cover you with his feathers.
He will shelter you with his wings.
His faithful promises are your armor and
protection. (Ps. 91:4)

You will not depend on your own wisdom.

Trust in the LORD with all your heart;
do not depend on your own understanding.
(Prov. 3:5)

You will extend love, joy, peace, patience, kindness, goodness, faithfulness, gentleness, and self-control.

But the spiritual nature produces love, joy, peace, patience, kindness, goodness, faithfulness, gentleness, and self-control. There are no laws against things like that. (Gal. 5:22–23 GW)

No matter what you go through, God's glory will be revealed through your life.

I consider that the sufferings of this present time are not worthy *to be* compared with the glory that is to be revealed to us. (Rom. 8:18 NASB)

I'm convinced that God, who began this good work in you, will carry it through to completion on the day of Christ Jesus. (Phil. 1:6 GW)

God is intentional with your life; all things are working for your good.

God causes all things to work together for good to those who love God, to those who are called according to His purpose. (Rom. 8:28 NASB)

God is not punishing you; He is fighting on your behalf.

For the LORD your God is going with you! He will fight for you against your enemies, and he will give you victory! (Deut. 20:4)

You have a future filled with hope.

"For I know the plans I have for you," declares the LORD, "plans to prosper you and not to harm you, plans to give you hope and a future." (Jer. 29:11 NIV)

You have everything you need to flourish.

By his divine power, God has given us everything we need for living a godly life. We have received all of this by coming to know him, the one who called us to himself by means of his marvelous glory and excellence. (2 Pet. 1:3)

Fear does not hold you captive.

For God has not given us a spirit of fear and timidity, but of power, love, and self-discipline. (2 Tim. 1:7)

You have peace that surpasses all understanding.

Don't worry about anything; instead, pray about everything. Tell God what you need, and thank him for all he has done. Then you will experience God's peace, which exceeds anything we can understand. His peace will guard your hearts and minds as you live in Christ Jesus. (Phil. 4:6–7)

You will put on the full armor of God every day.

Therefore, put on every piece of God's armor so you will be able to resist the enemy in the time of evil. Then after the battle you will still be standing firm. Stand your ground, putting on the belt of truth and the body armor of God's righteousness. For shoes, put on the peace that comes from the Good News so that you will be fully prepared. In addition to all of these, hold up the shield of faith to stop the fiery arrows of the devil. Put on salvation as your helmet, and take the sword of the Spirit, which is the word of God. (Eph. 6:13–17)

You can overcome everything with Christ.

But thank God! He gives us victory over sin and death through our Lord Jesus Christ. (1 Cor. 15:57)

Nothing will separate you from the love of God.

And I am convinced that nothing can ever separate us from God's love. Neither death nor life, neither angels nor demons, neither our fears for today nor our worries about tomorrow—not even the powers of hell can separate us from God's love. No power in the sky above or in the earth below—indeed, nothing in all creation will ever be able to separate us from the love of God that is revealed in Christ Jesus our Lord. (Rom. 8:38–39)

God's will will *be done in your life.*

Thy kingdom come, Thy will be done in earth, as it is in heaven. (Matt. 6:10 KJV)

In Jesus's name, amen.

ACKNOWLEDGMENTS

Phew! Thankfully, this book was completed before landing a new job as fashion editor at *Cosmopolitan*. Truly, digging deep in this way in order to write this book was one of the hardest things I've ever done, and I am grateful for all the solitude God allowed me in order to properly hone in. This time, the enemy didn't even wait for the release to come at me with full-blown attacks inspired by its contents! The level of emotional and spiritual toil was at its peak. And revisiting my 2020 journal and editing this work two years later forced me to go back to the place where I felt it all—where I thought it all. I'm so proud of myself for getting through it and for honoring this journey by leaving it as is. At times, I wanted to change certain parts because I was concerned with how the contents would be received, but ultimately, I know the Lord has led me to say all that is in here.

For the first time, He was the *only* one I went to for affirmation when I realized how vulnerable I felt, asking God,

Are You sure I should have this in here? I bore my heart, because He makes me brave, and I know He is covering me. There is absolutely no way I could've gotten through this process without the grace, attentiveness, and delicate nurturing of God, so I'd like to dedicate this portion to Him alone:

> *Lord, I want to thank You for seeing me for me. Even in my darkest seasons, You take note of my light. You show me daily that even in the moments I feel You are far away, You have never left my side. I'm grateful that I don't have to exchange words with You, You already know what's on my mind. I don't have to defend myself with You, You're already on my side. Big or small, You see every injustice and You fight for me. You crown me with love and honor in the way only You can. Thank You for seeing me for who I really am, for pouring out and for showing loving-kindness, understanding, and patience, and every day, showing me how to reign. I love You for who You are. Thank You for being my best Friend.*

NOTES

Chapter 1 Confessions and the Crown of Life

1. See Eph. 2.
2. See 1 Pet. 5.
3. See John 8:44.
4. This references the NIV translation.
5. John Piper, "Perfect Love Casts out Fear," Desiring God, May 26, 1985, https://www.desiringgod.org/messages/perfect-love-casts-out-fear.
6. John Pavlovitz, "Christians Shouldn't Try to Scare the Hell out of People," *RELEVANT*, October 28, 2015, https://relevantmagazine.com/faith/christians-shouldnt-try-scare-hell-out-people/.
7. This references the HCSB translation.
8. This references the NIV translation.
9. This references the EASY translation.

Chapter 2 Imposter

1. Mary Fairchild, "Eternity in the Hearts of Men - Ecclesiastes 3:11," Verse of the Day—Day 48, Learn Religions, June 25, 2019, https://www.learnreligions.com/eternity-in-the-heart-day-48-701890.
2. Hugh Whelchel, "Flourishing Begins with Filling the God-Shaped Hole in Your Heart," Institute for Faith, Work & Economics, November 17, 2014, https://tifwe.org/flourishing-begins-with-filling-the-god-shaped-hole-in-your-heart/.
3. Eccles. 1:2 (ESV).

Chapter 3 The Mute Button

1. Chandra Steele, "How Racial Inequalities Affect Influencers," PCMag, February 28, 2022, https://www.pcmag.com/news/how-racial-inequalities-affect-influencers.

2. Kerry Justich, "As Black creators gain sudden exposure on TikTok and Instagram, social media platforms begin to acknowledge inherent biases," yahoo!life, June 22, 2020, https://www.yahoo.com/lifestyle/black-creators-sudden-exposure-tiktok-instagram-social-media-platforms-inherent-biases-140131606.html?fr=sycsrp_catchall.

3. MSL Staff, "MSL Study Reveals Racial Pay Gap in Influencer Marketing," MSL, December 6, 2021, https://www.mslgroup.com/whats-new-at-msl/msl-study-reveals-racial-pay-gap-influencer-marketing.

4. Adam Mosseri, "Ensuring Black Voices Are Heard," Instagram, June 15, 2020, https://about.instagram.com/blog/announcements/ensuring-black-voices-are-heard.

5. See Matt. 18:15–17 and 5:9.

6. Colin Smith, "The Three Sins Behind Your Discontent," Unlocking the Bible, June 28, 2017, https://unlockingthebible.org/2017/06/the-three-sins-behind-your-discontent/.

7. R. C. Sproul, *Growing in Holiness: Understanding God's Role and Yours* (Grand Rapids: Baker Books, 2020), 86.

8. Sproul, *Growing in Holiness*, 86.

9. Sproul, *Growing in Holiness*, 86.

Chapter 4 The Purest Way

1. This references the NIV translation.

2. Seth L. Scott, "Why Does the Bible Say out of the Abundance of the Heart the Mouth Speaks?," Christianity.com, November 13, 2020, https://www.christianity.com/wiki/bible/out-of-the-abundance-of-the-heart-his-mouth-speaks.html.

3. Seth L. Scott, "Why Does the Bible Say?"

4. This references the NIV translation.

5. Tim Keller, quoted in Scott, "Why Does the Bible Say?"

6. Eccles. 9:3.

7. This references the NKJV translation.

8. James 4:4–8.

9. Matt. 22:37 (NIV).

10. John Piper, "Blessed Are the Pure in Heart," Desiring God, March 2, 1986, https://www.desiringgod.org/messages/blessed-are -the-pure-in-heart.

11. Ps. 24:6.

Chapter 5 A Walk with God

1. Tarah-Lynn Saint-Elien, *Claim Your Crown* (Grand Rapids: Revell, 2020), 154.

2. This references the NIV translation.

Chapter 6 Birthdays and Battlefields

1. David Guzik, "Daniel 10—Circumstances of the Final Vision," Enduring Word, accessed October 6, 2021, https://enduringword.com /bible-commentary/daniel-10/.

Chapter 7 The Shift

1. Joyce Meyer, *Battlefield of the Mind: Winning the Battle in Your Mind* (New York: Warner, 2002), xx.

2. Susan Gregory, "A Life Changing Experience," The Daniel Fast, accessed October 2, 2022, https://www.daniel-fast.com/project/a-life -changing-experience/.

3. *Merriam-Webster.com Dictionary*, s.v. "ideation," accessed March 8, 2022, https://www.merriam-webster.com/dictionary/ideation.

4. Heb. 4:12 (TPT).

5. Paul Coxall, "Repentance: A Change of Heart, a Change in Direction," Understanding the Gospel, July 22, 2020, https://understan dingthegospel.org/blogs/paul-coxall/repentance-a-change-of-heart-a -change-in-direction/.

6. Luke 17:21.

7. This references the MSG translation.

8. Dan. 10:13.

9. Guzik, "Daniel 10—Circumstances of the Final Vision."

Chapter 8 Defying Our Minds and Personalities

1. Joyce Meyer, *Battlefield of the Mind: Winning the Battle in Your Mind* (New York: FaithWords, 2011), 58.

2. Meyer, *Battlefield of the Mind*, 33–41.

3. This references the TPT translation.

4. Meyer, *Battlefield of the Mind*, 49–52.

5. Shawn Bolz, "Exploring the Prophetic with Steffany Gretzinger (Season 2, Ep. 32)," April 3, 2019, in *Exploring Series with Shawn Bolz*, podcast, 39:14, https://podcasts.apple.com/us/podcast/explor ing-the-prophetic-with-steffany-gretzinger-season/id1315785245?i =1000434011426.

6. "Architect Personality: INTJ-A/INTJ-T (What's the Difference?)," 16Personalities, accessed October 2, 2022, https://www.16person alities.com/intj-personality.

7. "Architect Personality: INTJ-A/INTJ-T (What's the Difference?)."

8. "Architect Personality: INTJ-A/INTJ-T (What's the Difference?)."

9. "2022 World Population by Country," World Population Review, accessed March 18, 2022, https://worldpopulationreview.com/.

10. "Current World Population," Worldometer, accessed March 18, 2022, https://www.worldometers.info/world-population/.

11. "Dig Deep with Dr. Jackie Greene | Topic: Thoughts TURN UP!," YouTube video, 1:54:02, posted by "Travis Greene," September 25, 2020, https://www.youtube.com/watch?v=9XDImneuQQY.

12. Exod. 17:15.

Chapter 9 Fear, Friendship, and Foes

1. Rom. 5:12.

2. John W. Ritenbaugh, "What the Bible Says about Satan's Influ-ence (from *Forerunner Commentary*)," Bibletools, accessed March 19, 2022, https://www.bibletools.org/index.cfm/fuseaction/topical .show/RTD/cgg/ID/1139/Satans-Influence.htm.

3. John 15:13.

4. Philip Yancey, "A Bow and a Kiss," *Christianity Today*, April 28, 2005, https://www.christianitytoday.com/ct/2005/may/2.80.html.

5. R. C. Sproul, "What Does It Mean to Fear God?," Ligonier Min-istries, January 12, 2018, https://www.ligonier.org/learn/articles/what -does-it-mean-fear-god.

6. Sproul, "What Does It Mean to Fear God?"

7. This references the NIV translation.

8. Sproul, "What Does It Mean to Fear God?"

9. "What Does It Mean to Have the Fear of God?," GotQuestions .org, November 22, 2006, https://www.gotquestions.org/fear-God. html.

10. Yancey, "A Bow and a Kiss."

11. John 4:23–24.

12. This references the TPT translation.

13. John Piper, "What Is Worship?," Desiring God, April 29, 2016, https://www.desiringgod.org/interviews/what-is-worship.

14. Piper, "What Is Worship?"

15. Piper, "What Is Worship?"

16. Piper, "What Is Worship?"

17. Yancey, "A Bow and a Kiss."

18. Rachel Ferchak, "How Your Personality Connects You with God," Cru, accessed March 22, 2022, https://www.cru.org/us/en/bl og/spiritual-growth/devotionals-quiet-times/how-your-personality -connects-you-with-god.html.

19. "Looking Beyond Disappointment," In Touch Ministries, April 1, 2022, https://www.intouch.org/read/daily-devotions/looking-beyond -disappointment.

20. John 8:32.

21. John 4:22.

22. Jon Bloom, "How to Have Intimacy with God," Desiring God, January 29, 2016, https://www.desiringgod.org/articles/how-to-have -intimacy-with-god.

23. James 4:8.

Chapter 10 Don't Forget Your Helmet

1. Eph. 6:12.

2. Gen. 3:15; Lev. 20:9; Ps. 7:16.

3. 1 Thess. 5:8.

4. 1 Thess. 5:8 (NIV).

5. Matt. 14:30.

6. Luke 1:34.

7. Gen. 17:17.

8. See John 20:24–29.

9. G. Campbell Morgan, quoted in Greg Laurie, "The Difference between Doubt and Unbelief," Harvest, July 21, 2016, https://harvest .org/resources/devotion/the-difference-between-doubt-and-unbelief/.

10. Colin Smith, "What's the Difference between Doubt and Unbelief?," Crosswalk.com, September 15, 2017, https://www.crosswalk .com/faith/bible-study/what-s-the-difference-between-doubt-and-un belief.html.

11. Greg Laurie, "The Difference between Doubt and Unbelief," Harvest, July 21, 2016, https://harvest.org/resources/devotion/the -difference-between-doubt-and-unbelief/.

12. Smith, "What's the Difference between Doubt and Unbelief?"

13. Smith, "What's the Difference between Doubt and Unbelief?"
14. v. 1 (NIV).
15. Smith, "What's the Difference between Doubt and Unbelief?"

Chapter 11 The Gift

1. Matt. 27:46; Heb. 2:12.
2. This references the NIV translation.
3. John 10:10.
4. JB Cachila, "3 Signs of Poverty Mentality," Christian Today, December 7, 2016, https://www.christiantoday.com/article/3-signs -of-poverty-mentality/102738.htm.
5. This references the NIV translation.
6. Saint-Elien, *Claim Your Crown*, 40.
7. James 2:5.
8. Rev. 5:9–10.
9. Eph. 1:7.
10. Rom. 5:17.
11. Col. 1:18–20.
12. 1 Cor. 6:19–20.
13. Gal. 4:5.
14. This references the ESV translation.

Chapter 12 Biblical Affirmation

1. Crystal Raypole, "How Many Thoughts Do You Have Each Day? And Other Things to Think About," Healthline, February 28, 2022, https://www.healthline.com/health/how-many-thoughts-per-day.
2. Prov. 23:7 (NKJV).

Chapter 13 Think like a Queen

1. Judg. 4–5.
2. 1 Kings 10:1–24.
3. Esther 4:14.
4. Esther 4:16 (NIV).
5. 2 Sam. 3:14–16.
6. 2 Sam. 6:16 (NIV).
7. "Who Was Michal in the Bible?," Got Questions, January 4, 2022, https://www.gotquestions.org/Michal-in-the-Bible.html.
8. "The One Who Seeks . . . Finds! | Pastor Steven Furtick | Eleva- tion Church," YouTube video, 1:03:49, posted by "Elevation Church," April 3, 2022, https://www.youtube.com/watch?v=CkYUUmuI-Mk.

Closing Chapter

1. Matt. 6:33 (ESV).

2. Jon Bloom, "Lay Aside the Weight of Discontentment," Desiring God, November 1, 2013, https://www.desiringgod.org/articles/lay-aside-the-weight-of-discontentment.

Tarah-Lynn Saint-Elien is the fashion editor of *Cosmopolitan* magazine, host of the *Dressed for Battle* podcast, and founder of Adorned in Armor ministry. A love-driven and multi-hyphenated millennial, her desire is to demonstrate how to live purposefully and dream big in unconventional spaces with Christ at the forefront. Crowned Miss Black New Jersey in 2018, Tarah-Lynn is the author of *Claim Your Crown* and *Love Letters from the King*. You can catch the Haitian-American beauty queen sharing her style, life, and encouraging words via Instagram (@iamtarahlynn), YouTube (Adorned in Armor), and www.tarahlynnadorned .com.

DISCOVER MORE RESOURCES
FROM **TARAH-LYNN**